HAUNTED
MAIDSTONE

HAUNTED MAIDSTONE

Neil Arnold

The History Press

*This book is dedicated to Charles Igglesden – the original chronicler of curious Kent,
and to Sean Tudor for his sterling research into the 'ghosts' of Blue Bell Hill*

First published 2011

The History Press
The Mill, Brimscombe Port
Stroud, Gloucestershire, GL5 2QG
www.thehistorypress.co.uk

British Library Cataloguing in Publication Data.
A catalogue record for this book is available from the British Library.

ISBN 978 0 7524 5922 6
Typesetting and origination by The History Press
Printed in Great Britain
Manufacturing managed by Jellyfish Print Solutions Ltd

Contents

This is a curious yarn that I am going to tell you.
'The House Among The Laurels', by William Hope Hodgson (*Carnacki the Ghost Finder*)

Foreword

WHEN, 2,000 years ago, the invading Roman legions landed on the shores of Kent, it must have been with some trepidation, even for Rome's battle-hardened soldiers. Known as Insula Sacra (the Sacred Isle), Britain was an island that lay beyond the limits of the Roman world. Shrouded in mystery and superstition, it was believed to be a land of ghosts, a place to which the Celtic peoples of Brittany consigned the souls of their dead. As they advanced inland into the frontier territory of Kent, the legionaries would have recalled Julius Caesar's foray into this land in 43 BC, from which he had returned to regale the Romans with tales of formidable tribes of wild, warrior peoples who daubed their bodies with blue dye; and the elevated caste of learned, austere magician-priests, who presided over arcane and bloody propitiations at the stone altars and mounds that studded their sacred groves and hilltops.

Dark and virtually impenetrable, the choking forests of the Weald harboured manifold dangers. They were the domain of wild animals – boar, bears and wolves; the refuge of bandits, and the haunt of spectres and demons. The routes of conquest therefore avoided the forests, and followed the navigable channels beside rivers and coastlands, over high ground and the native British track ways. The subjugation of the tribes of Kent, and then much of Britain, was to lead to 400 years of Roman occupation, in which time the Romans established their settlements and made their thoroughfares where the indigenous ones had once stood, thus establishing the basis for the network of towns and roads familiar today.

In his latest outing in Kent, in pursuit of the macabre and mysterious, Neil Arnold focuses on one such settlement and its environs. The County Town of Maidstone, first recorded by name in the tenth-century Saxon charters as 'Maeides Stana', evolved from a collection of Roman farmsteads and villas that sprang up where the Roman road from Lemanis (Lympne) to Durobrivae (Rochester) passed close to the River Medway. As may be expected of its long history, the borough of Maidstone has witnessed tumult, trauma and triumph aplenty, providing sufficient emotional charge for their echoes to reverberate down the centuries.

Penenden Heath, for example, served as a place of gatherings and executions from Anglo-Saxon times. In 1381, Wat Tyler marched from here into Maidstone at the start of the Peasants'

Revolt; and the heath served as the garrison for the defending Royalist army during the Civil War Battle of Maidstone, which raged in its streets in 1648. Suspected witches were hanged here in the seventeenth century on a knoll overlooking the heath, and felons continued to be hanged at this spot until the early nineteenth century, when the place of execution was moved to outside the gates of the new Maidstone Prison. In the town centre, in June 1557, as commemorated by a plaque affixed to the wall of Drakes Cork & Cask house, Edmund Allin, his wife and five others were burned for their refusal to take the Catholic Mass.

The creaking gallows, the people, and many of the buildings have long gone, but the locations and their ghostly memories remain. Join the author as he peels back the layers of history and legend to reveal Maidstone's oldest recorded supernatural occurrences; and as he explores the chilling and mystifying occurrences that continue to be reported in the town and in the surrounding villages, roads and countryside. All you need is warm clothing, a torch, and a stout heart!

Sean Tudor, 2011

Acknowledgements

I would like to thank the following people for their love, support, help and encouragement whilst writing this book: My mum Paulene, and dad, Ron; my sister Vicki; my nan Win, and grandad, Ron; my girlfriend Jemma; ; Sean Tudor; Joe Chester; Rod Stevens; Rachel Langley; Charles Igglesden; Ghost Search UK; Ghost Connections; Medway Archives & Local Studies Centre; Maidstone Town Hall; Hazlitt Theatre; Banks Wine Bar; Maidstone Museum; Frederick Sanders; Tom Atkinson; Kent Messenger; KentOnline; Historic Kent; The Why Files; the *Daily Mail*; Your Maidstone; *Fortean Times*, Corriene Vickers; Evelyn 'Missy' Lindley; *Medway Today*; Sharon Ramsden; the *Evening Post*. Also, many thanks to all the pub landlords and their staff for speaking of their resident ghosts and all at The History Press – Cate Ludlow, Beth Amphlett, Nicola Guy, Jenny Briancourt, Matilda Richards, and Kerry Green.

With a special thanks to Simon Wyatt. All illustrations are courtesy of Simon Wyatt, 2011.

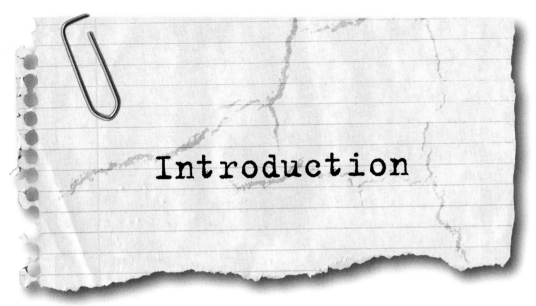

Introduction

Who's there? I shouted out in a voice about twice as deep as natural and with that queer breathlessness that a sudden fright so often gives one.

'The Searcher Of The End House', by William Hope Hodgson (*Carnacki the Ghost Finder*)

THE Borough of Maidstone is located in the county of Kent. Known as the 'Garden of England', it is situated just over 30 miles from the centre of London. In Kent, Maidstone has the highest concentration of population for a single town – approximately 140,000. The town's lineage can be seen as it appears in the Domesday Book as Meddestane.

Maidstone began life as a Saxon village with a population of around 250. Then from the tenth century it was owned by the Archbishop of Canterbury. By the thirteenth century it was large enough to be considered a town, although its status as a town wasn't awarded until 1549. As it was situated so close to the River Medway, Maidstone prospered as a centre for commerce. The river enabled produce to be transported to and from London via the waterway. The passing and local trade encouraged the businesses to expand. Market stalls were a common sight, littering the streets on a regular basis while fresh fruit and vegetables were sold in abundance. During the Middle Ages, a huge annual fair would take place, with people travelling from London and all over Kent to buy and sell goods. The town also harboured hundreds of small businesses, such as stonemasons, blacksmiths, bakers, brewers, and carpenters.

Although the dreaded Black Death affected the population during the middle of the fourteenth century, the population grew into the thousands rapidly (unbeknownst to many, behind Brenchley Gardens in the town centre sits what is known as Bones Alley – the site of a plague pit). In 1547 the King took control of the town, and by the seventeenth century more than 3,000 people resided there.

By the eighteenth century the population of Maidstone had risen to around 4,000. This number doubled by the end of that century. Around fifty years later, more than 20,000 people inhabited the town. Although, like many towns during this era, Maidstone was reasonably unsanitary, by the 1870s the streets had become cleaner and sewage systems were introduced. By 1858 Maidstone had its own museum.

During 1834 a startling discovery was made in Maidstone. An iguanodon – an extinct reptile from the early Cretaceous period – 20ft in length, and standing 13ft in height, was unearthed in a quarry which is now covered by the Queens Road. The creature was found in a slab of Kentish rag stone. The iguanodon now features in the Maidstone coat of arms. A wild ox, a woolly rhino, pterodactyls, plesiosaurus, ancient sharks, and mammoths have also been excavated in the town.

In 1901 Maidstone was given the power of electricity; by this time more than 40,000 people lived there. During the 1920s, the slums were demolished to make way for council houses, and in 1955 the Hazlitt Theatre was opened. By the twenty-first century more than 70,000 people resided in Maidstone.

Despite its history of epidemics and unsavoury slums, Maidstone's folklore has rarely been spoken of – until now. For many years people have reported strange encounters with ghosts and spirits in Maidstone's creaking buildings, rural pubs, and on old ground in the darkest corners. One of the most disturbing reports dates back to the June of 1206, and was recorded by Abbot Ralph of Coggeshall:

In the holy night of John the Baptist, all night thunder roared and lightning, terrific, incessantly flashed all over England. A certain strange monster was struck by lightning at Maidstone, in Kent, where, in the highest degree, the most horrible thunder reverberated. The monster had the head of an ass, the belly of a human being, and other monstrous members of limbs of animals very unlike each other. Its black corpse was scorched and so intolerable a stench came from it that hardly anyone was able to go near it.

Some theorise that the foul-smelling abomination may have been a wild animal such as an escaped bear (a bear pit used to sit in the vicinity of the High Street which meets the bridge), or was this fetid corpse a demon from another realm?

Dear reader, I do not ask you whether you believe in tales of ghosts, ghouls and monsters or not, but there is no doubt that after reading *Haunted Maidstone* you'll be more aware of the town's mysterious side. The hustle and bustle of the busy High Street today may give no inkling whatsoever to the events of the past, for very few people realise just how much blood has seeped into the soil of this town. From witch burnings to public hangings, to murders, Maidstone's folklore is rich in ghastly atmosphere. There are the classic ghost stories of Hollingbourne, Boughton Malherbe and Boxley, and the obscure cases at Aylesford, Bearsted, and the town centre. And, for the first time ever in print, a possible solution to the riddle of the 'Ghost of Blue Bell Hill', which delves deeper into the often repeated, yet inaccurate legend.

With so many tales of ghosts recorded in this book, please be aware that most of the buildings, and some areas of land mentioned, are private property, and those who wish to conduct ghost hunts should contact the owners first. So, grab a lantern, take a deep breath and join me in this supernatural jaunt through Maidstone's annals of the arcane. You won't be disappointed, but you'll certainly be chilled.

Neil Arnold, 2011

Maidstone Coat of Arms.

Presently through the thin gloomy red vapour I saw something that killed the hope in me, and gave me a horrible despair…

'The Hog', by William Hope Hodgson (*Carnacki the Ghost Finder*)

Haunted Maidstone

And, indeed, as you are all aware, I am a big sceptic concerning the truth of ghost-tales as any man you are likely to meet; only I am what I might term an unprejudiced sceptic. I am not given to either believing or disbelieving things 'on principle', as I have found many idiots prone to be, and what is more, some of them not ashamed to boast of the insane fact. I view all reported 'haunting(s)' as unproven until I have examined into them, and I am bound to admit that ninety-nine cases in a hundred turn out to be sheer bosh and fancy. But the hundredth! Well, if it were not for the hundredth, I should have few stories to tell you – eh ?

'The Thing Invisible', by William Hope Hodgson (*Carnacki the Ghost Finder*)

ALLINGTON

Recorded in the Domesday as Elentun, and in later records as Alynton, the village lies to the north-west of Maidstone town centre. Allington Locks attract many people, and each year visitors walk the stretch of the river to Teston.

An Anomaly at Allington Castle

An ancient order of Carmelites took over this grade I listed manor house in Allington in 1951, after it was converted from being a castle in 1492. The castle is stone built and was fortified in 1281; it even boasts a moat. In 1521, rebel leader Thomas Wyatt was born here. However, the castle is now privately owned.

Solomon's Tower remains as part of the original building of Sir Stephen de Penchester, and in this area the phantom of a servant girl is said to loiter. The girl has also been seen on occasion in the garden of the King's Tower. Much of the activity has ceased, but noises have been heard by people residing at the property, who reported footfalls echoing through the upstairs rooms as they sat down below.

Legend has it that the phantom maid was hanged, after drowning her illegitimate baby in the old, murky moat.

AYLESFORD

Aylesford is a large parish in the M2/M20 corridor between Chatham and Maidstone. Aylesford appears as Ægelesford in the Saxon

The Friars at Aylesford.

Chronicle, although the parish name has had a variety of spellings. The River Medway courses through the village.

Phantoms of the Friars

Dating back to the thirteenth century, the Friars at Aylesford is a tranquil setting and home to the Order of Carmelite monks. The first Carmelites, from the Holy Land, settled here and in 1242, under the patronage of crusader Richard de Grey, founded the priory on a small piece of land at his manor. Five years later, Richard of Wendover, the Bishop of Rochester, officially recognised the Order at Aylesford. The Friars website records:

> During the sixteenth century a tradition developed that St Simon Stock (died 1265), Prior General of the Order, had a vision of Our Lady promising her protection to those who wore the Carmelite habit, and the wearing of the scapular subsequently became an important Marian devotion. Some believe the vision happened at Aylesford but it is more commonly thought to have occurred in Cambridge.

Although the Friars is a very peaceful setting, the age of the buildings, which are several hundred years old, fosters the belief that there are a few resident ghosts. An area known as the Monk's Walk was once said, unsurprisingly, to be haunted by a monk who was imprisoned behind a wall. The figure is said to wander around in a white gown, his head downcast. This seemingly serene ghostly yarn then takes a dramatic twist, for it is said that suddenly, from behind a tree, two friars leap and apprehend the wandering monk. The victim is then gagged and dragged towards the Priory. The only noise heard being the muffled cries of the accosted monk. A few seconds later the ghostly trio completely vanish into thin air.

Charles Igglesden wrote of the monk in the third volume of his book, *A Saunter Through Kent With Pen And Pencil*, stating:

> ...it is said, one monk had offended his brethren in a manner that no ordinary death could expiate. Into the chamber – this old cell in the buttress – was he thrust; food and water sufficient to last him a few days were placed at his side, and then – the wall was bricked up. What a death! Slow, but sure.

Igglesden also wrote that many years later, the wall was pulled down and there lay the skeleton of the unfortunate monk, and so it was he who haunted the terrace. After the wall was taken down, the skeleton was given a proper burial and so, according to legend, the ghost no longer lurks.

Of the Old Carmelite Priory there is also a legend, written of by Igglesden, concerning a magical spring once found in neighbouring Burham. The 'waters were reverenced for the virtues they possessed', wrote Igglesden, who goes on to mention:

Not only would they heal the sick but a sinner might come here and heal himself from sin – for a consideration. Pilgrims came from all parts to test the power of the spring. But the Carmelites were too deep for the rustics of Burham. They obtained the consent of Richard the Second to run off the water to the Friars at Aylesford, an arrangement which brought it within their grasp and at the same time enabled them to take the tributes of pilgrims. They not only obtained a fine supply of clear drinking water, but filled their coffers too.

Vanished without Trace

There is a peculiar legend connected to the cellars that are said to sit below the priory. It was once believed that these rooms lead to entrances of subterranean passageways, said to stretch as far as Boxley Abbey. However, not many people dare venture into the blackness, for it was once rumoured that those who stepped into the depths never returned. One day, a brave man – a local fiddler – decided he would unravel the enigma and prove that the air of mystery surrounding the passageways was complete hogwash.

'When I enter,' he said, 'I will start to play my fiddle, and as I proceed through the darkness you will trace me by the sound.'

The confident fiddler slinked into the pitch-black passageway and began to play his tune. He strode off into the dark, and as those who stood by watched his form skip into the inky dark, their ears were met with one shrill scream from his fiddle and then a sudden, overwhelming silence. No-one dared follow the intrepid explorer, for fright had overcome them. The fiddler never returned and the entrance was quickly sealed up, leaving the adventurer alone to forever wander those cavernous tunnels.

Secret passages were said to wind beneath the priory.

The Fiery Spectre

Author Edward Verall Lucas gives mention to a dramatic road apparition from Aylesford, stating in his *Saunterer's Rewards*, of the Culpeper family (mentioned also under Hollingbourne):

> Sir William....a wild squire who lived at Aylesford, near Maidstone, not very far from Hollingbourne, is said to still be expiating a sin (merely killing one of his servants) by driving for evermore a coach and four down the avenue – on windy nights often destroying trees in his progress.

A horse and rider, possibly the same spirit, appear near the White Horse Stone, but both ghosts are said to be engulfed in flame.

The Paranormal at Preston Hall

Preston Hall exists today as a medical centre administered by the Royal British Legion, but in the past it was a delightful mansion dating back to 1102. The Culpeper family were associated with the house; during the reign of King John (1199-1216) it was owned by Walter Culpeper. The original construction was pulled down in 1848, two years after it had become a hospital. However, in 1992 Princess Diana opened the Heart of Kent Hospice on the site.

Like many ghost stories, there is a touch of romance about the tale pertaining to Preston Hall. An Elizabethan woman would often tiptoe out of the hall at night to meet her secret lover. However, on one occasion, a maid bumped into the man, and in a fit of jealous rage the Elizabethan lady murdered him, even though he and the maid had only crossed paths by accident. The ghost of a female in a long, flowing dress has been seen in one of the rooms which used to be a bedroom. It is also possible that another haunting – apparent by the sound of a couple arguing – could be connected to the tragic love story.

The Red Bull

This pub can be found at No. 1 Mackenders Lane, in Eccles, Aylesford. Although recent enquiries provided only scant mention of the ghost of an old man behind the bar, during the 1990s another ghost had been seen. A group of ten female friends (including the mother of the author) were eating in the pub one evening when suddenly a spoon was thrown across the table.

'Did you see that?' said one friend to another.

Preston Hall Hospital.

'Yes,' replied a woman called Myra. 'There's a little girl standing opposite who threw it.'

The girl was described as wearing a Victorian dress with puffed shoulders, and as having ringlets in her hair. The girl then vanished. Although the log fire was lit, the entire group described how the air had turned extremely cold.

The Ghost of Larkfield Priory Hotel

Larkfield, at Aylesford, has a long-standing ghost story that concerns the Priory Hotel, situated just over 3 miles outside of Maidstone. Larkfield is an ancient hamlet once referred to as 'Labroschesfel Hundret'. The hotel is a traditional old-character building, built during the mid-nineteenth century. It was constructed on Larkfield Farm and originally existed as Larkfield House, until it was destroyed by a fire in 1890.

The resident spectre has caused quite a stir and many ghost hunters have investigated the haunting. Charlotte is said to be a friendly spirit who once worked at the family home, serving under the Revd William Lewis Wigan. Revd William died in 1876 but his family remained until 1933. During this time, Charlotte was said to have fallen in love with the groundsman and to have married him, having fallen pregnant. Despite their long courtship, their relationship was frowned upon by many. Being made an outcast caused Charlotte great distress; under the strain she lost her baby. Her marriage then fell apart and once her husband left her, Charlotte fell into a black hole of depression and she eventually hung herself. Although no-one is sure where Charlotte took her life, several spots at the hotel are reputedly haunted. Is it Charlotte roaming the halls, lost in her own dark thoughts? During the 1980s, the owner of the hotel called in a medium to make contact with the unsettled spirit. The *Most Haunted* ghost hunting team also investigated the alleged haunting.

BARMING

The village of Barming lies to the east of Maidstone. It is mentioned in the Domesday Book as being divided into two parts – the east and the west, the former being urban, the latter of more rural air. The River Medway is the southern boundary of the parish. Saint Margaret's Church, in the village, dates back to Norman times.

The Red Bull at Eccles, in Aylesford.

The Bull Inn, at Barming.

BEARSTED

The Bull Inn

A pub has sat on a crossroads in the village since the sixteenth century. The site used to harbour a barn which sold ale illegally! From 1781, a pub sat on the site to dispense alcohol legally; however, like similar places in Kent a few centuries ago, the pub used to attract people who operated outside of the law, principally smugglers.

In the past, ex-occupiers reported loud shouting and unsettling feelings throughout the premises. Like most pubs, The Bull Inn has been prone to bouts of paranormal activity, such as glasses moving of their own accord and then being thrown across the bar, footsteps heard in the upstairs rooms and also the sound of whispers. Just over two centuries ago, a lunatic asylum was situated close by, and areas such as crossroads have long been considered cursed spots, often used for burials involving witches, or as locations for executions. Barming is also said to be haunted by a spectral horseman who rushes at cars in the more wooded areas of the village. The last encounter with the phantom horseman took place in 1971.

With over 10,000 inhabitants, the delightful and ancient village of Bearsted – situated 3 miles to the east of Maidstone – has housed some famous names, particularly the creator of the Scarlet Pimpernel – Baroness Thomas. The earliest traces of the village date back to 4000 BC, when farmers settled in the area. The fact that Bearsted is not mentioned in Domesday could simply be down to human error!

Ghostly Bears?

One very peculiar ghostly legend pertaining to the village may explain where the village got its name from. On top of the Holy Cross Church, at Church Lane, perched high above, are a few interesting figures, or 'gargoyles'. Some people believe these mysterious creatures to be bears, although to others the forms resemble dogs or something else entirely. Either way, author Charles Igglesden, writing in the fourteenth volume of his *A Saunter Through Kent* series, in 1920, stated:

Holy Cross Church, at Bearsted.

Some good folk of the village will tell you that these are the figures of bears – naturally bears in Bearsted – and I have heard others say they are actually intended to be lions. All this indecision is somewhat a reflection upon the skill of the sculptor, but he has at least given the old gossips of the village a chance to make their little joke. It is that the lions, or bears, or whatever they are, come down and feed in the churchyard when the clock strikes midnight. And the great jest of it lies in the fact that there is no clock in the church.

Another local author, Alan Bignell, in his book *Kent Lore*, adds slightly more detail, stating, '…one night of every year the three jump down from the top of the tower, stretch their legs a bit on the green and then always without being seen return to their perches to gaze over the surrounding roofscape with stony stoicism for another 365 days.'

A Creepy Clown?

Although possibly written as an April Fool's joke, in 2009 a bizarre headline appeared on the Kent Online website, asking 'Is this the Ghost Clown Of Bearsted', written by reporter Chris Hunter. Accompanying the story was an alleged photo, taken by a man named Grant in the White Horse public house, of a barmaid wiping clean the counter and a figure of a clown appearing in the foreground. The article read:

> Is this final proof of the legendary Ghost Clown of Bearsted Green?– White Horse regular Grant took this snap on his digital camera during an afternoon in the pub on Tuesday, and only realised later that he could have captured evidence of the mysterious phantom – said to only appear when the circus is in town.

In a remarkable coincidence, the snap coincided exactly with the arrival of John Lawson circus, who were that afternoon setting up on the green next to the pub.

The White Horse pub – haunt of a phantom clown?

According to legend, the phantom is that of Victorian jester Stitches the Clown, who died laughing after being shown the secret to perfect pratfall by an ancient clown guru. But the secret died with him – and now the spirit of Stitches returns every year hoping to pass on the secret to the next generation of clowns.

The Cobham Manor Incident

Situated within walking distance of Bearsted Station is Cobham Manor, equestrian centre and livery. It can be accessed via Water Lane and isn't far from the ancient trackway known as Pilgrims Way.

In 1985 several horse riders were doing a circuit within the paddock. Among those riders was Janet Emmot who, for the first time since being a teenager, was back on a horse. Janet's ten-year-old daughter Kirsten had mounted her horse and husband Martin was filming the day as a memento. With finger poised over the 'record' button, Martin waited as Janet and Kirsten slowly made their way along the fence-line, which was flanked by thick undergrowth. Martin filmed proudly, and after the dusk had long since settled the family went home. The next day Martin went

to work and Janet sat down to watch the video, but got the shock of her life.

'There it was, clear as clear,' she said from her Bearsted home. On the video, as recorded by Martin's 1980s Canon video camera, was Janet and Kirsten, on horseback, slowly trotting along the pathway; but behind them, seemingly in the undergrowth was a figure … but not just any figure.

'Martin rang me and I said jokingly, did you realise there's a ghost on the video ?' Janet said.

The video appears to show a Quaker type figure, or possibly a seventeenth-century preacher or Pilgrim Father, with white hair, dark clothing and a white cravat. The eerie apparition stands in the scrub as the riders slowly trot by, completely unaware of the figure standing so close to them.

Barry Hollis, the picture editor for the *Kent Messenger*, froze the image to check its validity. He said at the time, 'The moving image was frozen on a Sony video player using the still frame mode. I used a Nikon 801 35mm camera with an 80mm F1.8 Nikon lens to focus on the Sony Trinitron television screen. The exposure was 1/15 secs at f4, using Fuji 400 150 daylight negative film.'

Cobham Manor Equestrian Centre.

The film was difficult to dispute. Unless someone had somehow sneaked into frame, without the knowledge of those present, there is no way of explaining the darkly-adorned figure. The wraith is standing just a few feet from Janet and her daughter, yet they said there was no-one nearby. Even television experts at Vinters Park studios, in Maidstone, could not explain the image. One expert even asked Martin, 'Did you realise that the previous time you panned past the spot, there's what appears to be a head coming out of the ground?'

Janet was extremely spooked by the presence on the tape, even though she has always had a strong scepticism towards ghosts.

On Weavering Street, where it meets Ware Street, in Bearsted, there is said to be a ghost of a horse and rider. The rider allegedly fell from his horse and snapped his neck. Martin also recalled a story from a few years previous, stating:

> One winter's morning I took a horse up to the fields. It was about half-past four in the morning. There was no moon. I got to the crossroads and stopped to make sure there was no traffic. A voice called out, 'Are you real?'

'Yes,' I replied. It was my neighbour Barry King from up the road. He then said, 'It wasn't you who frightened old Charlie the other morning was it? He could hear his horse breathing and clip-clopping but he couldn't see a thing. He thought it was that ghost.

Whatever the belief in ghosts, there exists some evidence which is very hard to disprove, and the case of the Cobham Manor ghost is one that has stood the test of time.

Ghost on the Green

The Oak on the Green is a gorgeous pub in Bearsted dating back to 1665. The pub website states that:

> ...in an agreement between Daniel Birkman a distiller, a Thomas Buffield and Christopher Longley, a gentleman of Bearsted. Mr Longley was paid £200 for all that messuage or tenement not known by the signe of the Oake Inn, one stable, two gardens, one orchard, one piece or parcel of land belonging containing estimated 2 acres.

A further history is on display in the 'Olde Smoking Room' at the Oak. Local rumour says that the kitchen area was once used as a holding gaol for the local courtroom.

The pub is said to be haunted by a little girl, and as recently as October 2010 a few odd happenings have taken place, mainly concerning the window in a rarely used room, which is always opened by an unseen presence.

The Fox & Goose

Dating back to the 1600s, The Fox And Goose at Weavering Street – 2 miles from Maidstone Town centre – has had only a small amount of what could be deemed paranormal activity. Glasses have been known to fly off shelves and upstairs plugs have been switched off.

The Oak on the Green.

BLUE BELL HILL

The *Medway Today* of 4 May 2001, ran the headline, 'Weird accolade for local haunt', in reference to a magazine named *Bizarre*, which, in an article titled 'Weird Britannia League', claimed that the village of Blue Bell Hill was the weirdest in Kent. Kent came eleventh in the league of weirdest counties.

Blue Bell Hill is a chalk hill a few miles short of Maidstone. It is a place of great history and is part of the North Downs, which overlook the River Medway. During both the eighteenth and nineteenth centuries, the hill was quarried for chalk, but in the 1970s it was spliced by a dual carriageway. Local researcher Sean Tudor states:

Blue Bell Hill and its immediate environs have been a focus for human occupation and activity since before recorded history, long before the time of the Roman occupation when the first road was established here as a characteristically direct route to Rochester, where it joined the great Roman road of Watling Street.

The dual carriageway, the A229, was completed in 1972 to improve the flow of traffic, which to this day rumbles at great speed up both sections of the hill, now known as Upper and Lower Blue Bell Hill. Both of these locations harbour public houses, but the Upper Bell pub now stands empty.

Junction at the Lower Bell, Blue Bell Hill.

Blue Bell Hill is, as many magazines, news-papers, and books have surmised over the years, a rather strange place. Some places seem to harbour legends which quickly fade, and other locations experience brief ghostly phenomena to no real effect, and yet this tiny village, with its panoramic view across the Downs, appears to be a haven for the supernatural.

The Ghost of Blue Bell Hill – A Media-Created Legend?

On the night of 19 November 1965 a tragic accident took place on Blue Bell Hill. It involved two vehicles – one a Mark I Ford Cortina, the other a Jaguar. The two people occupying the Jaguar escaped with minor injuries, but three of the four women in the Cortina died; one instantly, the other two from their injuries – one was a bride-to-be, due to be married the next day. Doctors attempted to save her life but she never regained con-sciousness. Her husband-to-be sat by her side, and the next day people still turned up at the church (in Gillingham), expecting to see a wedding – many had not been informed of the bride's death. Ever since this fateful night ,a legend has existed on the hill, and for sev-eral decades many witnesses, usually motorists, have sighted a ghost, which they believe is one of the victims of that terrible crash.

Blue Bell Hill has long been perceived as a special place, its ancient chalk hills loom over the Downs, and in several secluded spots there are Neolithic stones displayed – the most famous being Kit's Coty House, which is situated in a field just below the Lower Bell public house and Little Kit's Coty, a mysteri-ous set of stones which have been bestowed the mystical title, 'The Countless Stones'. 'The Countless Stones' are believed to be the collapsed remains of a Neolithic stone burial chamber, and comprise twenty sarsen boulders, which in the past may well have been surrounded by another circle of stones. Legend has it that these stones – strewn about a small, enclosed area at the bottom of Blue Bell Hill, towards Aylesford – are impossi-ble to count, and should one do so then all manner of dark and sinister forces are said to be conjured. Of course, this is a contradiction in terms because if such stones are impossible to count then how on Earth would one know the consequences of a successful count?!

Author Charles Igglesden, in the Aylesford section of his third volume, of *A Saunter Through Kent With Pen And Pencil*, mentions a far more bizarre legend regarding the stones, stating:

> It is said that nobody can count them… and I must confess that upon visiting the place with three friends the other day, each of us counted the stones and brought out a different total – anything between

Photo of the crash which took place on Blue Bell Hill, 19 November 1965. This incident spawned an inaccurate legend.

seventeen and twenty-one. Many, many years ago a certain baker of Aylesford determined to arrive at a correct solution, so he appeared on the scene with a basket full of tiny loaves. Round the pile he went carefully placing a loaf on each stone. So far so good. Next he proceeded to count the loaves and place them in his basket. One, two, three, he picked up and so on, until he reached the last. In a voice of triumph he stooped forward and was about to call aloud the fatal number when with a gasp he fell dead! There is a variation in the story by which the baker, upon counting the stones afterwards, found one more loaf than he brought with him – a weird freak ascribed to the Evil One.

It was rumoured that in 1836 'The Countless Stones' were to be destroyed and used for paving at the barracks at Sheerness. Thankfully they still remain.

Kit's Coty House, meanwhile, is an eerie sight to behold, for it remains concealed from public view by an ancient pathway which runs alongside it. This dark, foreboding avenue may well have been a trackway used for the transport of bodies – nowadays it is a well-worn track frequented by ramblers.

Kit's Coty House is a burial chamber; it juts out from a field on the left of the pathway, about 100 yards up the track. It stands out like an imposing set of gargantuan and disfigured goal-posts, and legend has it that the main capstone, which sits on the two main stands – and a large backing stone – was positioned one dark and stormy night by several witches! In the book *Kent's Capital*, authors B. Prescott Row and W. Stanley Martin wrote of the house as a 'massive stone dolmen', its two sides measuring 7ft by 7½ft and 8ft by 8½ft feet, with a weight of 8 tons and 8½ tons respectively. The flat stone across the top was said to measure 12ft by 9¼ft, with a thickness of 2½ft and a weight of over 10 tons. Kit's Coty House is said to be older than Stonehenge, and adds to the mystery of Blue Bell Hill and its ghost stories. In her book *A Steep High Hill*, Edwina Kissick mentions that the name Kit's Coty, according to a Miss Glover, may have derived from Celtic *ked coed* meaning 'tomb wood'. Many years ago the tomb was covered by a 250m-long barrow and the burial chamber was at the south-eastern edge of the mound. In 2002 a television programme called *Scream Team* sent a handful of ghost hunters to the spot, and a few of them, along with a psychic medium, claimed

Kit's Coty House.

'The Countless Stones', or Little Kit's Coty House.

to have sensed a presence akin to Roman soldiers and peculiar lights. Many years ago, the field which harbours the stones was said to have been the site of a bloody battle. There is also rumour that the clashing of swords and sounds of horses' hooves have been heard in the area.

Charles Igglesden spoke of the origination of the upstanding stones as a complete mystery, but added:

> There are various theories about the origin of this old monument, one that it marks the spot where Catigern was slain and buried, the other that it is of more ancient date and was an altar erected by the Ancient Britons and used by the Druids for human sacrifice.

In the area, a great battle between Horsa and Vortigern was rumoured to once have taken place. Kent was the prize, and as the armies sprawled across the Downs an epic war ensued. Horsa was killed and Hengist carried off the slain hero. Some claim that the ghosts of Horsa and Vortigern still appear on the slopes around Kit's Coty, their shadowy forms wielding weapons and continuing their epic battle.

Author Rupert Matthews, in his book *Ghost Hunter Walks in Kent*, wrote:

> Local legend has it that after he was killed at Kit's Coty, the body of Horsa was brought here (to the area which houses the White Horse Stone) for burial by his grieving brother Hengist. The body was buried according to pagan customs of the early English. Then Hengist painted the stone blood red and on it drew the figure of a prancing white horse. The symbol was taken up by Hengist's son Oisc and so became the symbol of the Kings of Kent.

The mysterious stones go hand-in-hand with Blue Bell Hill's most extraordinary mystery – its ghost. Since the late 1960s, it is said that a girl, around twenty to thirty years of age, has appeared on the hill, and on cold and blustery winter nights has hitched a lift from passing motorists. On each occasion – according to this often repeated urban legend – the woman has vanished from the passenger or backseat. Several motorists have claimed that the woman they've picked up has mumbled few words, including the address to which she asks to be taken. Once the woman has

On this stretch of road many people have claimed to have picked up a phantom hitchhiker.

vanished, some of these spooked drivers have driven to the address the girl gave, only to be told, often by the parents of the girl, that she died many years ago. Researchers, journalists, and local people believe that the forlorn apparition is the spirit of the already mentioned bride-to-be, possibly searching for the love she never wed, or the destination she failed to reach.

This makes for a great ghost story, but the following encounters are far more strange than those which have embedded themselves into the local folklore. In fact, the tale of the 'phantom hitchhiker' in general is now very much an accepted legend across the globe, with similar reports coming from as far and wide as the United States, South Africa and Israel. However, as you are about to read, the Blue Bell Hill 'legend' has more substance and appears to have deep-rooted origins in historic events that pre-date the 1965 crash.

For more than twenty years, Sean Tudor, who moved to Maidstone in 1981, has exhaustively researched the high levels

Sean Tudor, expert on the ghosts of Blue Bell Hill.

OLD CHATHAM

of weirdness on the ancient hill. He has collected many tales concerning the ghost, as well as looking into weather conditions, natural phenomena, and other minute details connected to the stories, in the hope of fathoming this bizarre riddle. Strangely, despite such methodical research and many encounters reported by shocked eye-witnesses, Sean has found only seven cases in which motorists have actually picked up a girl on the hill.

The seven cases recorded by Sean are as follows. An Aylesford businessman (who wished to remain anonymous) stated that in 1967 or 1968 he and a girlfriend were travelling southbound towards Maidstone. A young woman, standing at a stretch above the Lower Bell, flagged the motorist down. He stopped the car and she climbed in the backseat, but when the driver turned to ask the woman where she wanted to go she had vanished. The man's girlfriend was extremely frightened by the encounter.

Richard Studholme was a guitarist for the band Chicory Tip. He claimed that he was the victim of a cruel hoax when one night, during the 1970s, he was driving in the region of the Lower Bell and stopped to pick a young woman up. She wished to go to West Kingsdown, but asked Richard if he could go to an address at Swanley after he had dropped her off, to tell her parents that she was safe. Richard dropped the

lady off at her requested spot and proceeded to the house in Swanley. When he arrived, at a late hour, he was told by the man who answered the door that his daughter had died several years ago in a car accident. There is a slightly alternate version of this tale, in which it is alleged that the girl was picked up and asked to be taken to Bridgewood, near Walderslade Woods. Studholme stated that after he took the girl's case:

> …she said very little, but asked if I would call at her parents' house at Swanley, further along the route to London. It wasn't until some months later that I read in a Kent newspaper of other strange happenings at the spot, that I began to believe I had driven a ghost in my car. I touched the girl. I took her bag from her and helped her into the car…

In 1971, James Skene was driving after midnight towards Maidstone from Blue Bell Hill, when a girl suddenly appeared in front of his vehicle. Despite being tired after a long day at work, he was alert enough to swerve to avoid the woman. Mr Skene then asked the lady if she wanted a lift. The woman slipped into the back of the car and asked to be taken to Chatham. Although frustrated by her request – as he'd already driven from that direction – he obliged and gave her a lift, but when he reached the location the girl got out of the car and vanished.

In July of 1974 came one of the weirdest encounters. Maurice Goodenough gave a different kind of lift to a different kind of girl on the hill. He claimed to have hit a young girl, who was around ten to thirteen years of age, but wrapped her in a blanket and lifted her to safety on the grass verge. Oddly, Maurice then drove to the police station without the girl, but when he returned there was no sign of her.

On 19 November 1974, the Evening Post covered the story of the ghost with the heading, 'Drivers beware of the phantom of the hill', supported by this sketch by Nigel Nelson.

In 1968, a couple from Sittingbourne, travelling to Maidstone, gave a lift to a woman who asked to be dropped off at an address in the town. The woman vanished from the backseat upon arrival.

Around the same time a chap, who worked at Rochester Airport, was driving from his home at Bearsted; heading up Blue Bell Hill, he stopped to give a lift to a woman. By the time the witness had reached the Upper Bell the woman had disappeared.

The final report of a phantom hitchhiker from the hill will be held back and told of in the section, 'Will the Real Ghost of Blue Bell Hill Please Stand Up?' – not only to keep you in suspense but to prove that the ghost of the hill is not connected to the 1965 crash.

As you have read, most of the alleged witnesses have picked up a girl who appears to be in her twenties, with the exception of the man who hit the girl. Oddly, on another occasion, a couple driving in the vicinity of Blue Bell Hill believed they had hit a similar young girl. However, since the 1960s, there have been far more disturbing encounters on the hill.

In the October of 1968, a Mr Chester was pushing his bicycle up the now disused slip road which runs next to the Upper Bell public house from the A229. He'd had a tiring day in Maidstone and was eager to get back to his Walderslade home as the storm clouds began to gather. Suddenly, as Mr Chester looked up ahead, he noticed a young woman emerge from the bushes on the left and walk towards him. Despite the weather being cold and damp, he noted how she wore a summery dress which clung to her; her matted hair crossed her face and she stared straight at him – a detail noted by several motorists which will be touched upon shortly. As the woman neared, she veered to the side, and as the witness looked back she vanished.

During the 1970s, a woman named Joy said that she was driving down the hill one dark, wintry night, when just a few feet ahead a woman dressed in a white gown appeared. The figure stepped out in front of the vehicle, and as Joy braked hard, the figure seemed to slink backwards from the car and vanish. Joy did not claim this figure wore a bridal gown, although it must be said that a few years after the 1965 crash no-one expected to see a ghostly bride on the hill. On 12 September 1977, the evening

news reported that an insurance broker named Barry Collings and his friend Stephen Pope were driving up the hill, when they noticed a girl standing by the side of the road. The woman was wearing a white evening dress which appeared to be dishevelled and she carried a handbag. Her hair was long and blonde. Despite the fact that it was a cold and blustery night, she appeared eerily still, even her hair failed to move in the gusts. It was as they neared that both men felt something strange was going on, and they sped away believing the girl was a ghost.

The two most famous cases concerning the Blue Bell Hill spirit are certainly far removed from the hitchhiker legend. At around midnight, on 7 November 1992, Ian Sharpe was travelling down Blue Bell Hill towards Maidstone. As he reached the Aylesford turn-off, on the southbound carriageway of the A229, he noticed a woman up ahead standing by the roadside. As Ian neared her she stepped out in front of the vehicle. He described her as wearing a light-coloured coat and having

The slip road next to the dilapidated Upper Bell pub, where, in 1968, a Mr Chester saw a ghost girl.

fairish hair, a round face and big, gorgeous eyes. Those eyes locked with his as he hit her, the vehicle skidding to a halt. When Ian went to check under the car he found no sign of the woman. Afterwards, Ian rushed to the local police station to report the accident.

Two weeks later Chris Dawkins was driving through Blue Bell Hill, in the vicinity of the Robin Hood Lane junction, not far from the crematorium, when a woman wearing a red scarf ran out in front of his Toyota. The woman looked at Chris as his bonnet struck her. Absolutely terrified, Dawkins got out of the vehicle but was shocked to find she'd disappeared from the road. Thinking she'd run off somewhere without him seeing, he hurried to a nearby phone box and called his dad who drove to the location. Whilst waiting for his father, Mr Dawkins then thought that maybe the woman was underneath his vehicle but was too unnerved to look. When Chris' father arrived he could find no trace and when the police searched the area they too found no body.

From this point the 'legend' of the ghost of the hill came to the fore. The encounters of the seemingly very genuine witnesses were reported in the local press, albeit with several inaccuracies, so it was up to Sean Tudor to siphon out the facts from the fiction – if facts can at all be applied to eye-witness reports of ghosts! However, the witnesses, when questioned by police, and by Sean, all believed they'd hit a very real woman. More than twenty people have reported encounters with some kind of female ghost in the area of Blue Bell Hill. It was commonly held by the press, and most other people, that the ghost was that of the tragic bride. However, the events of the proceeding year put pay to that theory.

The Old Hag

In 1993 a terrifying episode took place on Blue Bell Hill, which in turn threw the entire mystery into an even more bizarre realm. The Maiden family were travelling up the hill on the clear night of 6 January at 12.45 a.m. They were on their way home to Rochester.

Five people were in the vehicle: Malcolm Maiden was driving, his wife Angela was in the passenger seat, and in the back were Mrs Maiden's mother, their young daughter, and a friend of the family. They had turned northward onto the Old Chatham Road further up from the Lower Bell crossroads. Halfway up the hill the road bends to the right, and it was here that a figure crossed from the right to the left. However, this was no ordinary ghost, if there is such a thing. As the vehicle slowed, Mr and Mrs Maiden observed a huddled figure adorned in dark, old-fashioned garments. The apparition wore a tartan shawl and a bonnet, but immediately the couple thought that what they were seeing was the result of a belated Halloween prank.

'At first I thought it was somebody in a fancy dress costume,' Mrs Maiden remarked.

However, when the car headlights illuminated the figure in all its ghastly glory, the couple realised that what they were seeing was some kind of hideous, haggard old crone that came to within 4ft of the car. The vile hag-like spectre had black, beady eyes, a wizened face and a mouth agape like some pitch cavern. And then the figure rounded on the vehicle.

The 'old hag', another of Blue Bell Hill's ghosts.

'Oh my God!' gasped Mrs Maiden's mother from the backseat.

A horrible hissing noise filled the car and the spectre, carrying a spray of twigs, shook its bundle furiously. Malcolm pulled the car away, the witnesses feeling as though they were part of some weird horror movie scene.

Oddly, the night before this incredible encounter, another witness, whilst driving in the same area at roughly the same time, claimed to have seen the same decrepit crone.

Since these two encounters, confrontations with the hag-like apparition have been scant. In 2003, a young couple witnessed the spectre. At the time no-one knew who this ghost could have been, but after delving into the history of the hill, Sean Tudor believes there may be some connection to a local reclusive woman who once resided in the area. This lady may well have been called Mrs Apps, although this cannot be confirmed; but legend has it that this strange old woman was often seen roaming the woods around Blue Bell Hill, collecting firewod in the thickets. Locals were spooked by this lady and a handful of people spoke of her and how she would frequent the woods at night. Not many people were brave enough to walk the woodland pathways during the night in case they encountered the old woman, who often used to warn ramblers away from the area and state that she was some kind of guardian of the hill. Is it possible that when this old lady finally died she continued to roam the old hill on dark nights? Where else could this terrifying apparition have come from?

A Tom Atkinson once spoke of a legend which did the rounds at his school, in reference to an old woman on the hill. Tom stated that many kids knew a ghost story in which it was said that an old crone would wander the backwater roads with one or two phantom hounds on a leash. The hag would let these fierce, frothing beasts veer into the road causing vehicles to swerve to avoid them. Another legend, of a less sinister nature, from the hill, mentioned how the old woman would sit in an old cart and safely guide travellers up the hill.

Whoever this old crone is, it's unlikely we will get to the bottom of the mystery. Sean Tudor has looked into various complex possibilities which are deep-rooted in the realm of mythology, and these suggestions, which are plausible, are far too complicated to list here, or feature in any newspaper headline. Even so, one can hardly imagine the series of encounters many drivers and travellers have had on that old hill, and whatever you believe, one thing is for sure, Blue Bell Hill is a very weird place, and this can be confirmed with the next batch of tales.

Will the Real Ghost of Blue Bell Hill Please Stand Up?

The Blue Bell Hill 'ghost' appears to be a sum of varying complex parts, or indeed a cauldron of possibilities in relation to more than one haunting. However, the object of this segment is to finally unravel the rich tapestry of intrigue and hopefully shed some light on who the actual 'hitchhiker', or road apparition is. Sean Tudor is writing a book on the Blue Bell Hill ghost, which looks in-depth into the ghosts on the hill, and whilst researching his major work he shared some vital information.

This information has never been published before anywhere in the world and could, once and for all, answer the riddle as to who the young lady on the hill was. However, firstly we must travel back to 1934. In the previous segment there was mention of seven strange cases in relation to motorists who had allegedly picked a girl up on Blue Bell Hill. The seventh case can now be revealed, proving that the ghostly girl is not connected to the 1965 crash.

In 1934, a man was travelling on his motorcycle in the vicinity of the Lower Bell crossroads one night at 11.00 p.m., when he saw a girl standing in the middle of the road. He stopped for her and she hopped onto the pillion seat, requesting to be taken to Church Street in Burham, the direction which the witness had come from. However, casting his frustration aside the man took the woman to her destination and dropped her off, but when he turned his motorcycle around, there was no sign of the lady.

Now, some may scoff at such a report and remark at its vagueness, which is understandable. The witness may well have picked up a real girl who slipped into the darkness by the time he'd turned his bike around. However, there is a possibility that the witness was one of the first on record to pick up a ghost girl in the area of Blue Bell Hill, and this incident, although as circumstantial as so many others, could help solve the mystery.

Now we head further back in time to 6 August 1916. Twenty-year-old Emily Trigg was in her twelfth week as a maid, working and staying at No.36 Maidstone Road, Rochester. After finishing work she would walk to her mother's house at Providence Row, Blue Bell Hill, an address which no longer exists. On this particular Sunday, Emily wore her pale dress and white hat, as she was

Is the legendary ghost of Blue Bell Hill that of a servant girl named Emily Trigg? (Illustration by Simon Wyatt)

visiting her widowed mother, Kate, for a spot of tea. It was around 3.15 p.m. and Emily began the long walk up Maidstone Road towards Blue Bell Hill, which would take in the region of forty-five minutes to one hour. Emily never made it.

Catherine Cooper, who was Emily's mistress at the workhouse, thought Miss Trigg must have been ill and stayed at her mother's, but her mother eventually enquired at the workhouse the following Tuesday; bringing both women to the realisation that Emily was missing. The police were told of Emily's mysterious disappearance, made even more peculiar by the fact that Miss Trigg was hardly the type to go gallivanting off without notice. Of course, as the town was in the midst of the First World War there were much greater demands for the police. Even so, Emily still did not show until six weeks later, when her body was discovered on Thursday 21 September by greengrocer John Jennings, who had been picking blackberries with his two children in the woods at Bridge Wood, where the Bridge Wood Hotel now sits at Walderslade.

Church Street, at Burham. In 1934 a ghost girl was dropped off here.

The remains were completely decomposed. Some hair was still evident; a side comb was attached to the strands; a necklace found nearby was confirmed as belonging to Emily. A track leading to the spot where the skeleton lay revealed Emily's bonnet. Also close by was a photo of Emily's boyfriend, George Harris, who was a private in the Royal Surrey Regiment. He was eliminated as a suspect because on 6 August he was in hospital in Shoreham. At the time, police believed that a soldier may have been responsible for Emily's death. The most bizarre aspect of the case was the fact that the body had rotted so quickly in such a short space of time.

There appeared to be no traces left by the killer, although it looked as if Emily had been choked to death, because deep in her gullet was found a piece of material ripped from an under garment.

The only minor clue to the possible identity of the killer emerged when it was reported that Emily had been seen with a soldier that afternoon, and two weeks before her disappearance she had mentioned to her mistress that she had met a soldier. It was not something widely known at the time because Emily did not wish for rumours to be spread.

An inquest into the death of Emily Trigg took place in Chatham Town Hall and adjourned until 9 October whilst police carried out further enquiries, all which drew a blank. At the time there were no forensics or DNA testing and so the enquiry met a dead end, the jury returning with a verdict of 'found dead'.

Ten days later, a Mr Charles Hicks, a gunner in the Royal Garrison Artillery at Winchester, was arrested for connections to the murder of Emily Trigg. Gerald Hinks, who wrote of the case in *Crimes That Shook Medway*, stated, 'Charles Hicks said he was perfectly innocent and he had been brought there by mistake. In fact he seemed more concerned about the prospect of having prison food and asked to have his money returned to him so that he could pay for his own food.'

The following Tuesday, members of the public crammed into court to await the outcome, but a Superintendent Rhodes said there was no evidence against Hicks and he was discharged.

But what has the murder of Emily Trigg got to do with Blue Bell Hill and its ghost? Well, it may be a shot in the dark, but Sean Tudor, and myself, believe that Miss Trigg could well be the missing link, or a vital piece in the jigsaw, to reveal the identity of the young lady who has been seen/hit on Blue Bell Hill. Could the ghost of the hill, for decades connected to the 1965 crash, actually be that of Miss Trigg? Whilst there appears no reason as to why Miss Trigg would run out in front of vehicles, there is a far stronger case for her being the Blue Bell Hill ghost than the bride-to-be who died in the 1965 road crash. For a start, Miss Trigg would certainly have known the Blue Bell Hill area, and several anecdotal reports mention a girl around twenty-years of age, with brown hair and big brown eyes (all three apply to Emily), in a pale dress and wearing a bonnet. There have been mentions of a ghost in a pale blue dress and bonnet in the Bridge Wood Hotel at Walderslade, near where Miss Trigg was killed in 1916. Also, and rather spookily, Miss Trigg is buried at Burham Church, at the bottom of Church Street; maybe the girl picked up in 1934, who asked for a lift to Church Street, wasn't looking to get home, but instead wanting a lift ... back to the grave! Shudder!

Finally, some would argue that if Emily Trigg is the ghost of Blue Bell Hill, then why did she appear, in one instance in 1992 (Dawkins), not far from the crematorium near Robin Hood Lane? Well, after methodical research, Sean Tudor found that Providence Row, where Miss Trigg lived, was in fact a stone's throw from the phone box from which Chris Dawkins phoned his dad after knocking a young lady down.

Steve Hook, a local 'sensitive', said that on a visit to Blue Bell Hill, he had sensed a girl, around nineteen-years of age, standing at the bottom of the steps leading down towards Kit's Coty. He stated that the woman wore a chambermaid or waitress type outfit and had a white type of cap on her head. He also mentioned her name as being Maria – Emily Trigg's middle name was Maria – and that she was of Italian extraction (this is unconfirmed); also that she had been murdered in the vicinity of Blue Bell Hill. He also connected a soldier and the name George to her (George being the name of her boyfriend).

Certainly, Blue Bell Hill and its road-ghost have, for many decades, chilled the spines of those who have either alleged to have picked up the girl, or indeed knocked the girl down. It has even frightened those who are connected to someone involved in an incident with the apparition, while captivating and terrifying anyone who reads about the ghost. It makes for a fascinating story, and many have come to their own conclusions, but hopefully, after reading this segment, you'll be open to the possibility that the ghost is probably not connected to the terrible accident of 1965, and that such a tragic crash and its legend were tied together by local media. Even if Miss Emily Trigg is not the ghost of Blue Bell Hill, Sean Tudor has done a mighty fine job bringing another tragic case to the attention of the unknowing public. Mind you, if the ghost of Blue Bell Hill is Miss Trigg, which we believe is very likely, then to say we have shed new light on an old ghost story is the understatement of many a foggy decade. Rest in Peace Emily.

Hounds on The Hill

Folklore really does offer up some extraordinary cases. As if the levels of strangeness around Blue Bell Hill are not high and com-

Emily Trigg is said to buried in this churchyard at Burham. Did she hitch a lift back to the grave in 1934?

plex enough, we come to an entirely different set of ghosts – Hellhounds.

Throughout mythology there have been legends of phantom hounds – not ordinary ghosts of deceased pets, but fearsome, frothing, shaggy-coated, fiery-eyed monster dogs – said to prowl remote lanes at night. Such canine terrors were said to guard treasure and accompany lonely and weary travellers, often leading them to death, or astray into the dark woods. These calf-sized dogs exist the world over, especially in the UK where they go by names such as Black Shuck, Stryker and Padfoot. Some are said to burst into a ball of flames, others vanish into thin air, and some drag chains around their necks. Cerberus was the three-headed dog of Hades, and Garm was the watcher at the gates of Helheim, the Norse realm of the dead.

However, not all of these ferocious omens of doom are black in colour or confined to murky, ancient myth. On 22 January 2001, at 10.35 p.m., a Mr Flynn was driving through Blue Bell Hill. It was a cold and blustery night (as it usually is when these things happen!) and as he reached the footbridge that crosses near to the Aylesford turn-off, a white-coloured, Alsatian-sized dog ran across the road at great speed. The motorist slammed hard on the brakes, his knuckles turning white as he gripped the steering wheel. His front wheels locked, but a stunned witness was alert enough to see a Mercedes Benz travel-ling at quite a speed down the hill towards the creature. The ghostly-white dog seemed to accelerate and cleared the road; heading under the central reservation and out of sight. Mr Flynn drove home, convinced he had seen a spectral hound.

Similar apparitions have been seen at Dode, near Meopham, Tenterden, near Ashford, and Greenhithe near Dartford and also Boxley. (*see* Boxley sections).

Researcher Sean Tudor puts forward a complex theory regarding the Blue Bell Hill ghost and other manifestations which he connects to an old crone of mythology known as the Hekate. On his Road Ghosts website he writes:

> Known variously as the Crone Goddess of witches, the Veiled One, Goddess of Midnight, Queen of the Night, and Queen of Restless Ghosts, the Hekate was said to walk the highways of night (particularly at the dark of the moon), crowned with coils of wild snakes and wielding 'terrible black torches'. With her wandered a train of fearful ghosts: deceased humans, apparitions and dogs. Since crossroads were associated with her, these especially became the realm of these outcast and 'accursed spirits', which, in many cultures were said to include the restless spirits of suicides, those who had suffered a sudden or violent death, or those who had died childless. Some of these spirits merely frightened men; others were said to bring bad dreams, illness or madness.

The Ghost of the Lower Bell

During the 1990s, the Lower Bell public house, situated at the bottom of

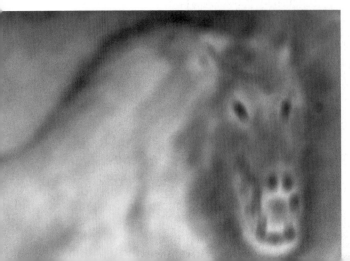

A white phantom hound is said to haunt Blue Bell Hill.

Blue Bell Hill, was run by landlord Lawrence Walker. He was interviewed for a paranormal programme called *The Why Files* in regards to a haunting at the pub. He told interviewer Dave Barrett:

> The Lower Bell is over one-hundred years old. It was a farm estate manager's house and there used to be stables out the back. One morning at 7.00 a.m., a week after we moved in, I was going down to bottle up in the cellar and something pushed me. I fell from top to bottom and broke my shoulder blade. Then, afterwards, the barmaids would tell me the gas had gone, I would go downstairs and the gas had been turned off. It should only be hand tight but I'd have to get a hammer to turn it back on because it had been turned off so tight. Then the lights would go off and on for no apparent reason. There's always a sort of cold and wet atmosphere down there – very uneasy.

Gwen Legg, a psychic drafted in by the programme to investigate the haunting, commented, 'The cellar, like all cellars, is very cold, but I felt compelled to go to the end of the cellar and there was a feeling that I had to keep going back to that part.'

Lawrence Walker added that:

> There was a little boy of eight who was chained down in the cellar and died of hunger. His name was Henry and he was a stable lad. A lot of mediums have come and got the feelings down in the corner of the cellar. That particular area is always cold.

Gwen, when asked about the presence of the boy, responded, 'I don't think that he is there any longer, he's long since gone and progressed. I feel it is just the impression that he has left. As long as the cellar is as it is, the influence will remain.'

Thumper

The final ghostly creature said to haunt Blue Bell Hill is known as 'Thumper'. This terrifying bogeyman-type creature was said to roam a vast territory from woods at Walderslade to the more dense areas of Maidstone. It was the stuff of childhood nightmares, whispered around a crackling campfire or in school corridors.

The Lower Bell public house.

This spectre was said to appear in two guises. Firstly, as that of a gangly woman, with spindly legs and large feet, who is said to run through the woods of a night, making her presence felt but only known by the sound of her thumping feet. Secondly, there is the belief that 'Thumper' was in fact some kind of giant ghostly rabbit, created as some type of woodland spirit, again, only making its presence known by the thumping of one of its back legs.

What Dave Saw!

Dave, from Chatham, was a keen metal detector a few decades ago. His house was once littered with old bottles, dirty coins and many fascinating artefacts. On one occasion, during the 1980s, Dave and a friend decided they would try their luck in woodland between Blue Bell Hill and Maidstone. The area in question was, at the time, extremely dense undergrowth, peppered with brambles and knee-high thickets; it was inaccessible in places. They began their search one afternoon in the hope of unearthing a hidden gem. After a short while concentrating on the ground and waiting for the 'bleep' of their trusty tool, they both sensed a presence and an eerie feeling of being watched. Dave looked up and in the distance, but ever so clearly, could see a figure in dark garb. The figure was male and he appeared to be standing in a thicket. Dave had his suspicions and thought that maybe it was a landowner spying on them from the shade of the trees. Both men decided to approach the gentleman and enquire as to his presence, but the closer they got the more eerie things felt, especially when they noticed his clothes. Dave commented, 'It was like seeing Oliver Cromwell!'

The figure wore a dark hat circled by a black band, and in the centre was a buckle of sorts. He wore a white shirt fronted by a long black tie and over this he wore a black coat, its darkness mingling with the black knee-length trousers which melted into knee-high white stockings. The trousers glinted at the waist with a buckle. The footwear of the gentleman was obscured by the dense bracken, which he rather oddly stood in. Dave and his friend stopped and stared at the man, who gradually began to fade into nothing, as if he had never been there in the first place. Both witnesses, with a chill down their spine, approached the thicket and noticed how impenetrable it was, and this spooked them even more.

Dave was a brave man – used to spending hours metal-detecting in gloomy old places. However, on this occasion he left the area, no longer bothered about the possibility of finding a treasure or two, but instead unnerved by the Cromwellian figure who had observed them from the foliage.

If you want to visit the haunted locations of Blue Bell Hill, then try the monthly Blue Bell Hill Ghost Walk run by Neil Arnold. It takes place on the second Sunday of every month. For more details visit: www.bluebellhillghostwalk.blogspot.com

There was once rumour of a giant, spectral rabbit-monster on Blue Bell Hill.

BOUGHTON MALHERBE

In 1870, Boughton Malherbe was, in the words of John Marius Wilson's *Imperial Gazetteer Of England And Wales*, described as:

A parish in Hollingbourne district … on the verge of the Weald … Post Town, Lenham, under Maidstone. Population 408. Houses 79. The property is divided among a few. The manor belonged, in the time of Henry III, to the Malherbe family; passed to the Wottons, of whom was Sir Henry Wotton, whose life was written by Isaac Walton; passed again to Sir Horace Mann, the correspondent of Walpole; and belongs now to the heirs of Earl Cornwallis…

Possessed?

The Historic Kent website mentions:

It was at Boughton Malherbe in 1574 that seventeen-year old Mildred Norrington, known as the Pythoness of Westwell, was tried before Thomas Wotton and George Darrell. Mildred's 'possession by the Devil' attracted a lot of interest in Kent at the time. She was a servant girl in Westwell where prayerful efforts were made to cast out the devil who, however, roared his

Boughton Malherbe, neighbouring Grafty Green.

defiance at the lot of them and became so violent that poor Mildred had to be held down by four strong men. When he calmed enough to speak rationally, he blamed an old woman called Alice, who also lived in Westwell, saying that he had lived at the old woman's house, shut up in a bottle, until the woman had sent him to Mildred, with instructions to kill the girl because she did not love his mistress, Alice. After more prayers, the Devil was finally persuaded to evacuate the girl's body and leave her in peace. Later, though, Mildred confessed she had faked the whole 'possession' and gave a demonstration to show that she could do it at will.

Judging by legend, it appears that Mildred Norrington gave up the act of tomfoolery, for it was said that had her demonic voices and acts continued, she would have been taken to trial at Boughton Place on suspicion of being a witch. No-one knows what happened to Mildred after she was teased into confession by Wotton, but her fifteen minutes of fame are now assured in the annals of folklore.

A Classic Ghost Story … or Two!

In his privately published *Psychical Research in Haunted Kent,* ghost hunter Frederick Sanders bathes The Old Rectory at Boughton Malherbe in anonymity, simply stating, 'The haunted rectory in question is situated in the Kentish Weald. It is a picturesque residence dating back to Tudor times. It has, for several generations, been a rectory; before this, upon reputation, a monastery; before this a manor house.'

The Old Rectory, according to legend, is one of Maidstone's most haunted properties. A hunch-backed monk in a grey habit has, in the past, been observed in one of the upper rooms, and on one occasion the wife of

The Old Rectory is said to be haunted by a phantom grey monk.

a former rector saw the apparition in broad daylight. Her sighting was confirmed when her daughter saw the same grey figure one evening. The first sighting of the monk was sometime between 1600-1650; he was allegedly last seen, according to Sanders, in 1938. This final encounter, involving the former rector's wife, was recorded as follows:

One evening in June [1938] I was adjusting my hat in the bedroom mirror before going out for a walk. It was a glorious day, with the sun shining brilliantly. The bedroom is at the end of the haunted passage, where it turns left to continue to another part of the house. The door of the bedroom was wide open. From the doorway you can see all the way down the passage, which is some thirty yards in length. The mirror in the room is placed so that the passage can be viewed for the whole of its

length in the mirror where it is reflected. While I was putting the finishing touches to my hat I saw a curious figure move silently across the end of the passage, from the stairway leading to the upper parts of the house, and enter the haunted room opposite the stairs.

It was the figure of the reputed grey monk! The shoulders were hunched and the figure was not much over 5ft in height. This mysterious apparition – I could not make out the features at the distance – was attired in the habiliments of a monk – long grey dress and grey cowl or hood. I thought it might have been my daughter playing a game and called out to her by name, telling her not to creep about so silently as to frighten one, in such a preposterous get-up or disguise. I immediately went along to the haunted room, but found it empty. The figure of the grey monk had disappeared. I soon afterwards ascertained that my daughter was not in the house at the time, but outside in the front garden waiting for me to finish dressing and come down and join her!

The woman's fifteen-year-old daughter had a frightful experience whilst in her room at the end of the haunted passage. The girl was pampering herself and turned to face the door and saw the elbow and lower arm of a person dressed in a coarse grey cloth. The arm moved but then vanished immediately afterwards. The girl was very brave and rushed quickly into the passage, but there was no sign of a presence.

It was also rumoured that the small dog belonging to the family was always too afraid to step into the haunted area.

Another former rector of the parish was often kind enough to allow local vagrants a bed for the night in the building. It was believed that the rector often did this to test the veracity of the legend, but no man would ever stay in the room for more than one night, often reporting they felt ill at ease.

The Old Rectory had another bout of strange phenomena too. On one occasion the wife of the rector (the lady who saw the grey monk) reported how

> One day, while I was in the kitchen, one of the bells connected with the front door rang. I went to the front of the house but no-one was about. At the time the house and grounds were deserted – except for myself – then who had rung the bell? Was it another ghost connected with the house?

The rector's daughter, who witnessed, the arm of the grey monk at close quarters spoke of another apparition said to haunt the building. She told Frederick Sanders:

> There is a legend of a very pleasant type of ghost…it is the ghost of the 'lady with the flowers'. It is said that she has been seen by former owners of the property, and that she has spoken to them! She walks about in a lovely dress of grey silk, and in her right hand carries a nosegay of flowers. She is said to speak words of comfort to those who have been terrified by the grey monk and the weird happenings here. She tells them: 'Please do not be afraid; I will take care of you!' At Christmas Eve she is said to write letters in the great hall and to read her Bible.

During a night in April 1940, Frederick Sanders investigated the property and ventured into the haunted room. At 10.05 p.m. Sanders reported that:

> Suddenly a weird manifestation [presumably of supernatural origin] appears opposite me at the far end of the room.

Descending through the dark are streaks and droplets of something which glows yellow-green, not unlike liquid fire. I want to get up from the chair on which I sit, but cannot. The liquid-fire rolls clean through the darkness and completely vanishes, as if into the wall. This fire came from the ceiling and, rolling down the wall about half-way twixt ceiling and floor, vanished. My heart beats a tattoo within me. The blood courses through my veins, but I am cold and shivering. I have been frightened – by seeing 'something' I had not even in my greatest hopes, and open mind, expected to encounter. The horrible feeling gradually subsided. I find I can move and rise to my feet, though my legs are unsteady and a general feeling of weakness pervades the legs and arms.

Sanders paid a second visit to the haunted property and after further investigation believed that the weird light effects he experienced were possibly some kind of illusion. However, he could not fully explain how the lights got into the room and so dismissed this notion.

In 1984, ghost hunter and friend of Mr Sanders, Peter Underwood, visited the Old Rectory with his wife and two friends.

The ghostly monk. (Illustration by Simon Wyatt.)

Underwood stated:

> We visited the haunted room and the adjoining small room; the bedroom where the rector's wife had seen the ghost in the mirror; the haunted passageway; the great hall; the kitchen and the gardens. Mrs Keen sleeps in the room where the ghost was mirrored and here, she told us, the wife of a former rector is said to have jumped to her death from a window. A ghost has been said to manifest here, looking over the shoulder of people who are looking into the mirror; but Mrs Keen told us that the only part of the undoubtedly atmospheric house that she feels may still be haunted is the end of the upstairs passageway [where the grey monk is supposed to have appeared], near the top of the stairway where, as she places her hand on the corner wall, she often has the impression that another hand is about to be placed over hers.

During the Second World War, a teenager, Dora Gregory, stayed the night at the Old Rectory with her sister. They had originally been staying at their uncle's house, but due to the falling bombs it was advised that they were sent elsewhere for safety. Although the night went without event, the following morning the two girls woke and headed off down the corridor. They noticed that one of the doors to another room was wide open and curiosity got the better of them and so they peeked inside. The girls were astounded to see a young girl in a nightdress plaiting her long hair at the foot of the bed.

When the teenagers went downstairs to breakfast they asked about the girl upstairs, but were told that the vicar's daughter was away. Dora and her sister also found out that a couple that stayed there once had sensed something dreadful in the powder closet.

Simply another ghostly tale to add to the list of spooks said to lurk in the Old Rectory at Boughton Malherbe.

BOXLEY

The village of Boxley is situated 2 miles north of Maidstone. It is mentioned in Domesday as 'Boseleu' and in the *Textus Roffensis* as 'Boxele' and 'Boxle'.

The Boxley Butler & Others

The Kent Online website states:

> Boxley Abbey was the scene of religious scams, with a statue of Christ reputed to be movable only by a person who had lived a pure life. In fact, the statue was made of paste, paper, wood and wire, and could even weep realistically when manipulated by unscrupulous monks. The abbey was destroyed by Henry VIII, but the vast Tithe Barn remains, along with a row of ancient cottages which were built to accommodate visitors and pilgrims en route for Canterbury.

Boxley Abbey was founded in 1143 by the Earl of Kent, William Ypres. It was used by an order of Cistercians who purportedly haunted it. Although the building has pretty much disappeared, witnesses at the abbey reported dark figures which glided silently over the ground.

Boxley House has allegedly been haunted since the 1950s, by the ghost of Thomas Sales, a butler at the house who committed suicide in 1898. In 1964 the house was owned by the Knowdens, who were given a cutting from the *Maidstone Gazette* in reference to a suicide and burglary at the property. A group of burglars allegedly ransacked the building and blackmailed the butler, who eventually hanged himself – but this appears to be an exaggerated version of the legend.

Mrs Knowden and her mother were standing outside the house one afternoon, admiring the decorating work being done at the time by a team of builders. Mrs Knowden glanced towards the bar area (the house was due to be opened as a club) when she noticed a figure move from the bar towards the stairs. She described the figure as being a short male wearing a cutaway coat, and having black, brushed back hair. Mrs Knowden's mother also saw the mystery gentleman. However, it wasn't until Mrs Knowden looked at the newspaper clipping that she realised she'd seen the ghost of the aforementioned butler. However, the newspaper report stated that he'd shot himself (not hanged himself) in the pantry.

The butler worked at the house for more than twenty years and was considered, by the locals, to be of sound reputation. However, when a burglary occurred – only two rugs were stolen – the police were puzzled. Had someone let the criminals in? Strangely, despite being of cheerful disposition, Thomas Sales' demeanour changed drastically. His wife stated at the time of the incident that her husband had seemed troubled by something. Shortly after, the butler was found dead in the pantry – he'd shot himself around breakfast time and was discovered by the cook. Rumour spread among the servants that Mr Sales believed that the police were suspicious of him and would arrest him for the crime, even though this was not the case. It appears that the seven men who broke into the property had blackmailed the butler and threatened to kill him if he uttered a word. This was confirmed when papers were found on the butler speaking of the men. Clearly Thomas Sales could take no more, and took his own life.

The butler's pantry was turned into a lavatory, and it's possible that the building work disturbed his spirit. On one occasion, two women staying at the hotel were walking down the stairs to the reception area when they reported that they were pushed by unseen hands. Fortunately, the women were quick enough to react and reach out for safety. Shortly afterwards a male guest had the same experience on the stairs.

A friend of the Knowdens, a Mr Cornford, mentioned that several members of staff had seen the ghost of the butler glide towards the stairway, and that he always seems to vanish near the lounge area.

The Man-Eating Phantom Hound of Boxley

Reports of phantom dogs, known as Hellhounds, as mentioned in the Blue Bell Hill segment, have been prevalent for many years, not only around Maidstone, but all over the United Kingdom. The Pilgrim's Way, an ancient pathway which runs from Canterbury to London, was said to, in the region of Boxley, have once been haunted by a giant hound, which has remained a rather obscure apparition embedded in the annals of local folklore.

The year was 1654 when the 'great dogg' was said to have savaged and killed a man, on what author Charles Igglesden described as, '…the upper road'. Although the mention is brief, and, allegedly, from Igglesden's *A Saunter Through Kent With Pen And Pencil*, there is no evidence to suggest it does appear in the volumes; it may simply have been information he received in a letter. Of course, such yarns sound like something akin to supernatural fiction, but consider also another sighting – this time in 1745 – on the Pilgrim's Way when a peddler was killed by a 'lean, grey hound with prick't ears', which at first appeared behind the man and his friend and then up ahead. Where the man was mauled he was said to have been buried.

In 1654 a ghostly Hellhound was said to have killed a man near Boxley. (Illustration by Simon Wyatt)

Broomfield.

Sometime during the 1800s, two men, including a Revd Edward, or Revd Edward H____, depending on sources, who recorded the encounter, were walking near to Maidstone towards Boxley Church when:

> …at a point where the road ascends… in its course, we paused to take breath, and look't back and were surprised to see some distance behind us, and standing on the way we had come, a lean grey dog with upstanding ears…I was struck by its size…it appeared as big as a calf.

Modern research points the finger towards an out-of-place wild animal such as a wolf or large cat, like a lynx or puma. For over a century, mysterious large cats have been sighted throughout Maidstone and the rest of the country. However, could a credible witness such as a Reverend have got his description wrong? The legend has persisted for centuries, so it is possible that a spectral hound did once roam around Boxley; but why such a manifestation appeared no-one will ever know.

BROOMFIELD

Situated 6 miles east of Maidstone and located just a short way upstream from Leeds Castle, this small village forms the civil parish of Broomfield and Kingswood.

The bells, the bells!

A village sign at Broomfield reads:

> This village sign depicts a church bell and the home in Broomfield of bell founder Joseph Hatch. From 1606 to 1635 Joseph occupied Roses Manor Farm. Joseph cast his early bells in Broomfield but it is likely that many of his later bells were

Was the phantom hound of Boxley a large, elusive 'big cat'? (Illustration by Simon Wyatt)

cast on his lands in King's Wood, in Ulcombe parish.

There is a strange legend connected to the bell which hangs in the parish church for it was once believed that such a bell was rang to frighten away storms, fires and pestilence. Also, demons were once said to trouble the spirits of the dying, and so to deter them the 'passing bell' was used.

BURHAM

Burham can be traced back to Roman times. There has been a settlement here since the Saxon period; the latter part of the village name, 'ham', meaning settlement. The fore-part of 'Bur' refers to 'Burgh', or what we now know as Borough. It sits at the foot of the North Downs and straddles the Pilgrims Way between Chatham and Maidstone. In his book *Around Historic Kent*, Malcolm John writes of a strange tombstone (now lost) in the grounds of the 'Old Church' – St Mary's. The stone has a twisted face on it and the words:

Behold Burham's Belle, a delight,
With her curls asymmetric and tight;
Let us hope that her Biz,
Was as straight as her Phiz,
And she kept like her Nose to the Right

This church, sitting at the base of Burham, near the reservoir, may hide another strange, ghostly secret, which can be read about in the Blue Bell Hill section.

Coach & Horses

Burham is allegedly haunted by a spectral coach and horses. In fact these kind of spirits seem relatively common around the Maidstone area. No-one knows who occupies the coach, but it is said to drift along the Pilgrims Way area and through Burham on the main stretch.

A Ghost in the Picture?

The Toastmasters Inn at Church Street, Burham is said to be haunted. The Burham Village website mentions a modern ghost story from the public house, about a mysterious photo which was taken on New Years Eve 2001. A local man named Keith Thompson took a snap of a boisterous group celebrating the New Year, but upon closer inspection the

Burham is said to be haunted by a phantom coach and horses.

photo on the wall in the background – which is a picture of an old corner pub – actually shows the smiling face of a woman. The lady in the photo is Mabel whose cottage used to sit where the cosy bar of the pub is. Mabel was a regular at The Toastmasters Inn and often used to sit in her own corner (near the photo) - which became known as 'Mabel's Corner' – and clean the glasses to help the landlord. After Mabel passed away, the pub purchased the cottage and turned it into the bar and second kitchen you see today; so maybe Mabel still likes to frequent the place. A plaque, in remembrance of Mabel and her special corner, was placed above the area where she used to sit, and since her passing there have been reports of a ghostly figure in the pub. Glasses have also reportedly moved of their own accord.

The Red-Eyed Apparition

In 1992 a bizarre, spectral figure was sighted in woods around Burham, by a group of men. The gentlemen were walking to a pub during the dark hours when suddenly, on a path ahead they noticed a pair of red, fiery eyes. Thinking someone was playing a prank, and attempting to prove their bravery to one another, the men reacted by shouting at the apparition, and as they approached they began to throw objects at it. However, one witness reported that the flint he threw seemed to simply pass straight through whatever stood up ahead on the pathway. The eyes then seemed to blink out and the men continued their journey for a few yards. When turning the bend, they were startled by the appearance of the eyes again, only this time they were just a few feet ahead but, clearly a few feet higher than their heads, suggesting these blazing eyes belonged to a very tall figure. With that the men yelled in fright and scrambled away, leaving the unknown presence to its nocturnal meanderings.

In 1974, a woman and her boyfriend were tending to a camp fire in woodland not far from Blue Bell Hill, when the lady, named Maureen, noticed a huge, hairy creature with glowing eyes, which stood only a few feet away. She observed how it blinked its eyes and stood far taller than her. The beast gradually melted away into the darkness, but Maureen was so petrified she ushered her boyfriend away from the woods and never told him of her experience.

Oddly, both of these terrifying encounters echo an obscure legend from Wouldham, a neighbouring village of Burham, where, during the early twentieth century, it was reported that a particularly hirsute man had prowled the overgrown pathways of the woods. The story was passed down from an elderly lady to her granddaughter who believed that the 'creature' was still spoken of in the area up until the 1960s.

COXHEATH

According to the Village Net website, the name Coxheath 'is possibly derived from the fact that a large number of soldiers were garrisoned on the heath from 1776 for 40 years.'

The Haunt of the Highwayman

The ghosts of highwaymen are relatively common in folklore and many parts of rural Kent are said to be littered with tales of these cloaked phantoms on horseback. The heath was a deserted tract of land up until 1756 and highwaymen were said to prowl after dark. It's rumoured that these dandy robbers still haunt the more isolated areas of the village and surrounding locations, although some of the vague ghost stories could also concern the fact that thousands of soldiers once camped in the village. They were waiting to be transported to the Americas. Maybe some of these soldiers have returned long after death for one more rest upon the heath.

Coxheath.; the haunt of spectral highwaymen. (Illustration by Simon Wyatt)

DETLING

Detling is a village in the Maidstone district, located on the slope of the North Downs.

A Half-Hinted Presence

The Ghost Connections team – Ian, Kim and Dave – investigated the little known and overgrown Binbury Castle. Situated close to the disused airfield and industrial estate, this construction was once a motte-and-bailey castle transformed into a manor house, which now, sadly, only exists in ruin. After a night of surveillance, and attempts at contacting a spirit, the team were only rewarded with the occasional clicking noise, an infrequent thud and a faint scrubbing noise, although Dave was apparently tipped from his chair by an unseen presence.

EAST FARLEIGH

The village of East Farleigh sits on the banks of the River Medway and has a beautiful medieval stone bridge, comprising of five arches.

The Horseshoes

Located on Dean Street, The Horseshoes is a lovely pub dating back a few hundred years. Recently, the assistant manager reported that one night, he heard noises down in the bar after closing time, as if someone was walking about. When he went to investigate there was no sign of anyone.

The Walnut Tree

This building, situated on Forge Lane, has been a pub since 1796, but the building dates back to 1528 when it existed as three cottages. It used to harbour a butchers and a bakers, but now this cosy pub, complete with inglenook fireplace and exposed beams, is the perfect place to snuggle up for an award-winning real ale.

The Walnut Tree, East Farleigh.

Like many haunted pubs, The Walnut Tree has a spirit which likes to move glasses and even remove them from the shelf, suspend them in mid-air, and then drop them to the floor. Stools in the bar have been moved around, pots and pans in the kitchen are mysteriously stacked up when no-one is around, and more recently customers have watched in astonishment as jugs hooked from the beams have begun to swing in different directions. The oddest activity was recorded a few years ago when several customers saw a face appear in the blackboard. Footsteps have been heard upstairs and figures have been seen to walk through walls. Some believe that these ghosts could well be those of hop-pickers. In 1849 forty-three pickers died of cholera in the village and a monument exists in memory of this.

Grafty Green

The small hamlet of Grafty Green, near Boughton Malherbe, endeared itself to writer Charles Igglesden so greatly that he wrote, 'Were I a poet I should write verse all around it', so intrigued was he by the 'click' of the two words in its name.

The Kings Head

Located on the Headcorn Road, The Kings Head has long been haunted by a famous smuggler known as Dover Bill (Charles Igglesden records the character as Dover Will from Bethersden whose real name was Else and was said to have been aided by a fellow named Christian). Bill was a local rogue who frequented the pub with his gang of not-so-merry criminals but when the Revenue confronted the rascal about his crimes, Dover Bill grassed on his buddies to save his own soul. Bill may have lost his popularity, but his gang lost their lives (all except Christian who escaped punishment and was said to have watched the execution take place). They were hanged at Penenden Heath. From then on Dover Bill deteriorated, haunted by his actions until his death, and so it is said that the smuggler now haunts the pub. Customers have, on occasion noticed the figure of a man exuding menace and also sensed an oppressive atmosphere when his spirit lingers.

The Kings Head.

A more recent landlord, named Mr Jackson said there had been no activity regarding Dover Bill's alleged spirit.

Igglesden however, in his twenty-sixth volume of *A Saunter Through Kent With Pen And Pencil* gives an alternate legend of the ghost stating:

> On one occasion the Excise officers suddenly arrived in the village just as Christian and Dover Will were carrying barrels on their shoulders. They made a rush across country until they reached Chilston Park, where they threw their loads into the lake and escaped. But Dover Will was hit in the leg and died, and some of the old people will tell you that his ghost still roams over the fields at night between Grafty Green and Chilston Park

Igglesden also states that the ghost of the village is in fact of Christian who is said to ride a white horse across the fields.

On the façade of the pub there is a sign commemorating smuggler Dover Bill.

Witches!

Sue Twitt and Sally Clark were two mischievous women who had a bit of a reputation for having supernatural powers. Sue Twitt was said, on occasion to spook local waggoners who swore blind that the 'witch' could, with a mere stem of straw placed in the road, stop an entire team of horses dead. The ghost of Sally Clark is reputed to haunt a footway through fields, for it was at a certain spot that the woman used to sit for hours.

On a Dark and Stormy Night

All good ghostly tales are better suited to nights of diabolical weather – lightning forks spearing from the sky, thunder rattling the windows, and hard rain pelting the cobbles. It is said that in the vicinity of the aforementioned Kings Head pub, there is said to race a spectral coach and horses, which hurtles past the inn and heads toward the church.

Some witnesses to the phantom vehicle state that the coachman is bereft of head and that screams can be heard emanating from the carriage, as if those contained therein are terrified by the speed of the coach in the treacherous weather. Above the entrance of the pub there is a sign depicting the headless coachman and his team of horses. Usually these type of ghost stories lack any modern relevance, however, the already mentioned Mr Jackson, once landlord of The King's Head, stated:

> One man I know quite well told me about it. He is a local gardener and when

Sign on The Kings Head pub depicting smuggler Dover Bill.

Another sign on The Kings Head pub, depicting the coach and headless coachman.

walking home from the pub late one night he passed the Old Rectory and suddenly heard the most blood-chilling sounds. It was the noise made by horses in their death throes mingled with the dying screams of passengers in the wrecked coach. The man was completely shaken by his experience and said that he had never heard anything so horrible in all his life.

HARRIETSHAM

Originally spelled Heriagierdeshamme, the name meaning 'Heriagdierde's water meadow', the village is 2 miles from Leeds Castle and sits between Maidstone and Ashford. Harrietsham is said to owe its existence to a series of springs situated at the foot of the Downs.

The Haunting of the Ringlestone Inn

Near Harrietsham is the several-centuries-old pub, The Ringlestone Inn (formerly Ringlestone Tavern) – 'the ring stone' (pertaining possibly to the ring outside, which is set in the wall and was once used to tether animals). A 1632 carving on an English oak sideboard reads: 'A Ryghte Joyouse and welcome greetynge too ye all'. The inn, built in 1533, was originally used as a hospice for monks, and then became an alehouse around 1615. Little has changed since the seventeenth century, making this inn a cosy place to drink and eat.

One of the more fascinating legends of the inn concerns the true story of two women, Florence Gasking and her daughter Dora, who used to own the place in the 1960s, and would often send rowdy customers packing by firing a shotgun at the ceiling! Last orders indeed! More accurately, it seems that any unwelcome folk would be warned off when coming face-to-face with the doublely-angry and double-barrelled shotgun duo! Those welcome at the pub would use a personal secret knock to enter. Florence and Dora retired from the pub in 1967.

The inn also has its resident ghost or two, as you would expect from such an old and atmospheric property. The spectre, possibly a

Above: The sign inside the pub.

Left: The very haunted Ringlestone Inn at Harrietsham.

male, makes itself known by stomping noisily about, as if wearing heavy boots. However, the mysterious noises could have many explanations; Peter Underwood, the great ghost hunter, in his *Ghosts of Kent*, wrote:

> Could this be the echo of a smuggler, stomping up the cellar steps at dead of night? Or a former landlord, straining an overworked heart? Or a robber, caught in the act? Or a lover, grown careless enough to be found out? Or an unsuspecting husband coming upon his wife and her lover?

The noise could simply be a recorded apparition taking one of its shoes off and letting it drop to the floor. And it is said to occur throughout the year; day or night; rain or shine. In his book *Haunted Pubs in Britain & Ireland*, Marc Alexander writes that the ghost:

> …could easily have been a comic from the old music hall days. From their sound the progress of the ghost could be traced to the top step where he halted, and then a few seconds later dropped a single shoe. One theory is that in life he was about to creep about the tavern in stockinged feet on some nefarious activity when he was caught by the landlord.

A strange humming noise has been reported on occasion in the pub and this is said to come from the mouth of a ghost named Stanley, who, it is alleged, worked as a farm hand. Investigators from Ghost Search UK picked up several energies from the inn. Two of these were a young boy and girl. The young boy was said to be the son of a former landlord. Many years ago he was alleged to have stolen a sheep from a nearby farm; although he did it to feed his hungry family, the result was a severe punishment – imprisonment or deportation! The parents were so worried about losing their son that they hid him in the house by bricking him up behind a wall (with a gap left to feed him through) so the authorities could not find him. Legend has it that the child soon stopped taking the food and, rather presumptuously, the parents thought him dead and decided to brick the gap up and move away from the premises. A rather harsh act when one considers there must have been easier means, by communicating with the boy to make sure he was still alive! And so it is said that the apparition of this young boy could well haunt the inn. Mind you, a young boy had apparently died many years ago in one of the upstairs rooms, and has been blamed for the moving of household objects such as toys and keys.

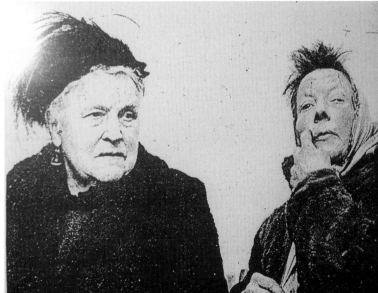

The pub was once run by a mother and daughter team who warded off certain customers by firing a shotgun!

There were also a few less defined ghosts such as a male who was said to have passed in 1753, and a woman named Mary Jane Cooper, who died of cholera in 1856 aged just forty-three.

As appears to be the case in so many modern ghost investigations, strange orb-like forms were picked up on pictures taken with digital cameras used by the researchers. Many paranormal enthusiasts, and indeed some experts, believe such orbs to be spirit forms. My personal opinion is that such forms are nothing more than particles, possibly of dust, not seen by the naked eye. Such orbs have only become prevalent in the digital camera age, where numerous haunted locations are said to be littered with such souls, which frequently appear on camera.

An elderly couple are said to haunt a specific corner of the bar area, and it is believed that in life they loved the pub so much that their spirits have refused to move on.

Many years ago, a highwayman named Elias Shepherd used to frequent the ill-lit and un-policed road outside of the old inn. Many such criminals would loiter in the shadows of the woods from Maidstone down to East Kent, and on remote lanes would accost coaches. There is a crossroads near the inn called Black Post Crossroads and at this spot it is said that many highwaymen were hanged. Author Janet Cameron, in her book *Haunted Kent*, states that such characters, '… were considered in league with the Devil and unworthy of being buried in consecrated ground'.

Fleeting figures throughout the surrounding countryside could well be the ghosts of those ghastly highwaymen.

Phantom Vandal

The ticket office at Harrietsham station is said to have once harboured a poltergeist, which, since the Second World War, has plagued the building. Some of the more superstitious folk who have experienced the activity claim that since a wartime stretcher has been removed from the wall of the building, a phantom vandal has manifested itself.

The Stede Court Spook

Stede Court and its ghost were written of by Charles Igglesden in the Harrietsham section of the eleventh volume of his *A Saunter Through Kent With Pen And Pencil*. Igglesden speaks of a ghost story from Stede Hill which has been passed down through generations. Many local people who knew of, or stayed at, Stede Court spoke of the ghost of a woman in a long, flowing, white silk dress. This mysterious lady often appeared near the blocked-up staircase which used to connect the billiard room with a bedroom above. Legend has it that whilst one of the Stede knights was away at war, his spouse had been entertaining another love. Upon returning to his home, the sire found his love in bed with another man, who fled the chamber and escaped, but the lady was not so fortunate. Her furious husband threw his unfaithful wife down the stairs and she was dead by the time she hit the bottom. The angry and cheated man put her body in an oak chest and was said to have buried it beneath the floor of the hall. Shortly afterwards, the man met a new love, married her and lived happily ever after, but on occasion it was rumoured that the ghost of his perfidious ex-wife roamed the mansion.

There appear to be no modern sightings of the female wraith, although there are a scant few who believe she makes her presence known by the rustle of her flowing gown. Others claim to have seen her pale form floating amidst the trees of the grounds, for she is now rumoured to be angry at her descendants for disposing of the estate, and so she refuses to haunt the chamber she so favourably frequented when she was alive.

Stede Court.

HEADCORN

Headcorn lies just to the south of Maidstone and is situated at the centre of the northern part of the Kentish Weald. It is accessible via the long main street from Maidstone towards Tenterden, and sits between both on the A274. Its name is derived from the Saxon meaning 'trees cut down by Huda to produce a clearing'. Although the meaning of 'Hudakaruna' could date back further to 'haed hruna', the Anglo-Saxon for 'bridge by the heath'. This has, over the years, changed to Hedekaruna in 1100, then to Headcorn.

A Personal Ghost Story

During the 1970s my father, Ronnie, and grandfather, Ron, were working for Mortley Plant Hire, and on one occasion were renovating a shop in the High Street of Headcorn; this building still exists. The structure is a listed building and its sloping floors gave the feeling of having one leg longer than the other! The building was in such a terrible state. The doors had no handles and bore string latches.

On this particular day my father and grandfather were working upstairs in the front room of the shop. The building was securely shut and the only door open was the one in the room where they were working. The string was tied on the outside of the door and not on the inside, so maybe you can guess what happened next?

All of a sudden the door slammed shut with a loud bang. There had been no draught and certainly no-one else in the building, but now my dad and granddad were locked in. Although they never fully attributed this strange incident to a ghost, my dad had to climb down through the ceiling in order to come back up to open the door from the outside.

It is possible that the unseen presence, which locked them in, did not like them being there and felt that its privacy had been invaded.

The Haunted Tree

There was once a ghost story attached to an old oak tree, said to sit among the forlorn graves in the grounds of an old church within the village. Many years ago there were two men who fell in love with the same woman. This love triangle was fated to have a tragic end; and so, one dark night, one of the men hid up in the old oak and as his competitor walked by, he sprung down and stabbed him. The victim was sent to Maidstone hospital where he eventually died. The woman was so devastated by her lover's death that she fell into despair and eventually died of a broken heart. Ever since her death, her pining soul has been said to wander around that old oak tree, hoping that she'll someday meet her lost love.

This same tree hides another spooky set of secrets, for it is rumoured that on certain nights goblins can be seen perched in the lower gnarled branches. What their motive is, no-one really knows, and it appears that no-one is brave enough to loiter in the area at night in case they should, not only be accosted by the leathery-skinned critters, but also encounter the female ghost.

In 1776 a terrible flood broke over land at Headcorn. Igglesden wrote that:

> The causeway leading to Frittenden and the farms over the river was impassable and the water came within a few feet of the base of the old oak close by the churchyard fence. Sheep and pigs were drowned and in some cases the inhabitants were for a time in considerable danger.

It's surprising then that there are no reports of ghostly animals from the village!

HOLLINGBOURNE

The name Hollingbourne is said to derive from Hola, an Anglo-Saxon/Jute leader who may have owned the area in the vicinity of the 'bourne', or stream. There are references to the village in the Domesday Book. A more folkloric explanation for the village name says that it derives from the fact that an abundance of holly trees used to blanket the village. Alternatively, the origin of the name could be that Hollingbourne was once known as Holybrook due to the stream which was once said to have lead to an abbey in the region of Leeds.

A Spook at the Station

In his book *Single Track Obsession: A Book of Extraordinary Railway Journeys*, author Rob Sissons writes of a strange encounter which took place in 1994 at Hollingbourne's rather remote station (Hollingbourne station was constructed in 1883). He reports:

> I had thought I was alone, but then I spotted the other traveller. He was wear-

Hollingbourne station.

ing a top hat and a Victorian frock-coat with a high collar. His skin was unusually pale but his lips were a deep red. Trust me to be getting on the same train as a weirdo, I thought. I walked about as far down the platform as I could. The strange gentleman just carried on gazing across the tracks. I wondered if he had been to a fancy-dress party the night before?

The old slam-door electric train crept into the station and I got on. Looking back along the platform, the Victorian gentleman was still there, gazing into space, making no effort to join the train. As we pulled off, I looked back and saw he was still on the platform. If he wasn't a ghost he must have been a mime-artist, but surely Hollingbourne station on a Sunday is not the best place to tout for business.

A Haunted House

Edward Verrall Lucas' *Saunterer's Rewards* gives mention to the Culpeper family of Maidstone, stating:

The Culpepers, as a race, once so powerful and numerous, seem to be extinct; as long as thirty years ago W.H. Hudson believed them to be so. But in their time they even gave their country a queen, although not too securely set on her throne: Catherine, granddaughter of Sir Richard Culpeper of Hollingbourne, whose daughter, Joyce or Jocosa, married Lord Edmund Howard. It was to marry the widow Catherine Howard that Henry VIII divorced Anne of Cleves, that unhappy 'Flanders mare', and having sentenced Catherine Howard to death, he espoused the fortunate lady 'who survived him', Catherine Parr.

Catherine Howard's ghost is said to walk in Hollingbourne Manor House, although there has often been some confusion as to which house in Hollingbourne she actually haunts, if at all. Ghost hunter Peter Underwood stated that the 'Colpepper' family inhabited Greenway Court; but it was originally held by the Greenway family. It was purchased

The haunted looking Hollingbourne Manor House has several ghost stories attached to it.

in 1572 by Francis Culpeper. It is said that Catherine Howard also haunts this old building. A few years ago, school children from the Hollingbourne Primary School interviewed many local people in reference to the local ghost stories, and many folk seemed sceptical regarding the Catherine Howard spectre. Some believed it was simply a deliberate fake to bring in tourists to Hollingbourne Manor House. Others believed there was no direct link between Catherine Howard and Hollingbourne to suggest the lady haunted the village. However, it is possible she may have been 'taught politeness' in one of the old buildings, but again, why she allegedly haunts Hollingbourne is a mystery.

The spirit of a small man has also been seen in Hollingbourne Manor House, and the sounds of the rustling of clothing have been heard on occasion.

Another haunted house is Eyhorne Manor ,dating from the fifteenth century, which is 5 miles north of Maidstone and close to Musket Lane. Bizarrely, Catherine Howard's ghost has also been linked to this property, but again, this appears to be nothing more than confused legend. Its most sinister spirit comes in the form of a slithering sound. A Mrs Simmons, who once owned the manor with her husband, spoke of the eerie unseen presence which sounded as though it was always approaching her. The slithering noise was also reported by other occupants. On one occasion Mrs Simmons was so perturbed by the sound that she fled into the garden. The couple also recorded that when they moved into the manor they found three marbles in the ashes of the original fire, a French water bottle and a pair of children's shoes.

During the 1940s, one of the cottages which then made up the manor was said to have been haunted. Not only were phantom footsteps heard, but a resident, a Mrs Brunger, mentioned how her four-year-old daughter kept asking her about the 'little old lady'. The child claimed that each night an old lady would enter her bedroom and read her stories. However, the words were

Eyhorne Manor near Musket Lane, Hollingbourne.

Several ghost stories are attached to Eyhorne Manor.

whispered so low that the girl would often complain to the mystery woman that she couldn't hear. On one occasion the girl's mother listened intently at the bedroom door and could quite clearly hear her daughter talking as if someone else was in the room. The mother was so spooked that she moved her daughter to another bedroom. At the time, a neighbour reported seeing a grey lady gliding through the hallway.

A ghost of a man in black was observed in the garden by Mrs Brunger, who, whilst tending to her flower beds one afternoon, got the shock of her life when she looked up and saw the spectre. The witness looked away for two seconds, but upon returning her eyes to the man, he had gone. She told ghost hunter Andrew Green:

> …there was nowhere for him to go except into my cottage and he hadn't gone in there. At one time a small black dog would visit us and he would sometimes stop in a particular spot of the garden and growl with all his heckles raised. There was nothing there, but he would be looking at the spot where the little man had stood.

The property appears to be riddled with ghostly activity. On another occasion the witness to the man in black spoke quite adamantly that she had seen a peg on the clothes-line fall to the ground and vanish. There was also a brief encounter with a man dressed in a green velvet suit, and voices from other rooms as if they were occupied by several people. The clinking of coins has also been reported, and in 1960 the ghost of a small dog walked straight through a door.

More recent owners, whilst restoring parts of the manor, reported that items of clothing and utensils would simply vanish, or on occasion the objects would rise into the air

and then drop to the floor, as if picked up and dropped by some invisible hand. Also, a woman who moved into the manor with her two children was often unnerved by their claims that they had heard someone walking on the stairs. This haunting went on for almost ten years.

The Phantom Horseman

Hollingbourne Manor House is mentioned with reference to a character named Duppa, who resided there during the seventeenth century. Duppa is blamed for the sightings of a phantom horseman said to ride around the area. Those that have witnessed the spectre claim it appears very solid, and the horse trots along quite calmly. The figure perched on the back of the horse wears a wide-brimmed hat (though sometimes he is headless), and the spurs on his boots jangle eerily in the still air. Only when the horseman vanishes, in the region of the gates of the house, are people startled to realise that they have in fact observed a ghost. There have also been reports of the apparition around Bearsted where some witnesses have claimed to converse with the ghost.

A spectral horseman, sometimes bereft of head, is said to haunt the lanes around Hollingbourne. (Illustration by Simon Wyatt)

Gethin's Ghost

Hollingbourne is also reputedly haunted by a Lady Grace Gethin who, during the seventeenth century was considered quite a catch among local gentleman. However, she was a whiter-than-white character, devoted to her faith. But but one Sunday afternoon, during a church visit, she was said to have stood abruptly with a jolt, screamed and collapsed. When Lady Grace finally came to, she spoke of a vision she had experienced, which eventually was carved onto her tomb (she died the next day). Her tomb sits in the parish church. The tablet reads:

> She was vouchsafed in a miraculous manner an immediate prospect of her future blisse for ye space of two houres to ye astonishment of all about her and being like St Paul in an inexpressible transport of joy thereby fully evidencing her foresight of the heavenly glory in inconceivable raptures triumphing over death and continuing sensible to ye last she resigned her pious soul to God and victoriously entered rest.

It's no surprise that Lady Grace is said to loiter around the churchyard, wearing a bonnet and adorned in an immaculate dress.

A Poltergeist

There is brief mention of poltergeist activity from the area of Lime Kiln Cottages, which, during the 1930s was plagued by an unseen phantom, said to throw cucumbers around the kitchen of the property.

The Spectre of Sugar Loaves

At No. 56 Eyhorne Street sits the splendidly named Sugar Loaves, a pub said to date back to the 1600s. It has been a pub since the 1800s, but before that it was a greengrocers. It is owned by Norman and Carol, who men-

The Sugar Loaves Pub on Eyhorne Street.

The Windmill on Eyhorne Street.

tioned that the premises are possibly haunted by a landlord who resided there forty years ago. A male figure has been seen flitting behind the bar, and on one occasion a customer reported that some unseen presence had constantly been digging him in the ribs. Now, this chap, according to the current landlord, was a big fellow who could look after himself, but the constant prodding by invisible fingers spooked him so much he left the pub.

The Windmill Wraith

The Windmill public house also sits on Eyhorne Street in Hollingbourne. It was built in the 1550s and began life as cottages; it is a former coaching inn. During the 1790s, the landlord was said to have been killed outside the pub after stumbling and hitting his head during a fight. Maybe the ex-landlord now haunts the pub, and is responsible for spooking the resident dog and also moving objects around the place.

The Manor Hall Maid

There is brief mention in local records of Manor Hall being haunted by a maid. Her ghost has loitered around the property ever since she drowned in the mill pond.

HUNTON

Hunton, situated 5 miles out of Maidstone, was once known as 'Huttingstone the hunter's town'. Ancient deeds mention Hunton as Huntington; the parish sits southward from West Farleigh.

The Hunton Hill Horror

On the 20 September 1985, at 11.30 p.m., a lorry driver named Peter Russell, whilst driving up Hunton Hill, was said to have hit a woman who was lying in the road. A police officer and a doctor were already at the scene and told Mr Russell that he had not killed the girl. They told him that they would take care of the matter and urged him to go home and rest. Peter, too traumatised by the incident, visited the local police station, but was told that there had been no accident and that he must have been the victim of some bizarre hoax!

An Obscure Haunting

In an issue of *The Spiritual Magazine* from 1872 there is a brief mention of an undisclosed haunted house at Hunton. It is spoken about by a Mr Thomas Grant of Shirley House, Maidstone, who comments on a strange rapping heard on the ceiling, and the fact that the house had been attracting much attention.

LANGLEY

Langley is a small village just outside of Maidstone. The parish church of St Mary is almost 300 years old and is situated next to a lake. The tranquil reserve of Abbey Woods sits close by.

A Whisper

On the Francis Frith website there is a photo of Rumwood Court in around 1955, and under it a comment from a woman stating:

> Rumwood Court was the country home of Lord Rootes (of motor-car manufacturing fame). During the war the house was used as a maternity home for army wives to have their babies. I was born there in August 1942. My mother said there was a 'whispering gallery' which was reputed to be haunted.

LEEDS

The village of Leeds is nestled 5 miles east of Maidstone. Less than 1,000 people inhabit the place, and yet each year thousands upon thousands of people visit the beautiful castle.

Leeds Castle, at almost 900 years old, is without doubt one of the most beautiful castles in the United Kingdom. It is listed in the Domesday and was raised in stone during the reign of William the Conqueror's son, Henry I.

It sits in a glorious setting with tranquil surroundings, including a peaceful moat, occupied by abundant wildlife, including its black swans, which have become the symbol of the castle. The castle existed as a Norman stronghold and has also been the residence of six medieval queens, as well as acting as a palace for Henry VIII. Although today the castle is a wonderful tourist attraction and also the perfect location for important meetings, it has also been the residence of three famous families: the St Legers, the Culpepers and the Fairfaxes. It was also owned for more than a century by the Wykeham-Martins. In 1926 it was purchased by the Hon. Mrs Wilson Filmer, who later became the Hon. Olive, Lady Baillie, who was an Anglo-American heiress of great fortune. After Lady Baillie died, the castle passed into the hands of the Leeds Castle Foundation. Thankfully, the castle has maintained its Gothic atmosphere, and stepping into each and every room one feels as if they have stepped through a portal in time, as rich tapestries, creaking libraries, exotic paintings and luxuriously designed

Leeds Castle, described as 'the loveliest castle in the world'.

bedrooms paint pictures of a past that doesn't seem too far beyond the reach of the imagination.

The Dog of Doom and the Wicked Duchess

Leeds Castle has one of the most fascinating ghost stories pertaining to an animal. For centuries, records have existed of encounters between humans and phantom animals. Some of these spectral creatures may be nothing more than recorded spirits of deceased pets, but the apparition of Leeds Castle could be something altogether more sinister.

Legend has it that a Hellhound, or phantom black dog, has haunted the castle since the fifteenth century. It may have come about after rumours that Henry VI's aunt, the Duchess of Gloucester, had, after the death of her husband – Humphrey, the Duke of Gloucester (who died in 1447) – become slightly unhinged and taken a ghastly, diabolical route into practising 'witchcraft'. At

the time, the Church, and certainly the local folk, were eager to condemn such practices. During 1450, the Duchess was imprisoned at the castle for her strange antics, but managed to avoid execution due to her connections to Henry VI. Whilst her very sincere and late husband had always been known as the Good Duke, the Duchess was bestowed the title of the Wicked Duchess. Whether her imprisonment was one of suffering, we'll never know, but it appears that the security of the outside moat and those stone walls acted more as a protection for her, and those that lived in the surrounding areas also felt safe in the knowledge that the Duchess could not escape and practice her alleged evil deeds.

It is no coincidence that the resident female ghost, said to float along the long corridors of the castle, is said to resemble the Duchess. Recent sightings of the wraith are few and far between, but her legend appears to exist in her strange connections to another, more ghoulish ghost.

The black dog of Leeds Castle has at times been rumoured to prowl the country lanes which wind round the castle. Others argue that the fleeting glimpses of a black creature can be explained by the more recent sightings of a big, black, slinking leopard, which has also been seen in the neighbouring villages. Reports of a creature, as tall as a man and with burning eyes, have also been tied to the Hellhound reports, which together walk hand-in-hand aside the whispers of the Duchess and her black magic conjurations. Over the years, like many reports of Hellhounds, the country over, such canine beasts have become the symbols of misfortune – omens of doom. It is said that should one look into the eyes of the black ghost dog, then surely that person will die or suffer a great loss. Others suggest that the hideous hound stalks lonely travellers of a night on remote roads and leads them astray like some tormenting will-o'-the-wisp. Whether this demonic dog was the product of the Wicked Duchess and her evil ways, we'll never know, but it seems unlikely that the lady could have, from the confines of her castle prison, commanded such a spectre to kill. If we look at an alternative version of the legend, it seems that we do not have to fear the Leeds Castle ghost hound as much as we first thought.

The Wykeham-Martins, who resided at the castle, prior to the First World War, spoke of a medium-sized retriever-type dog which used to materialise and then vanish. Others at the time recorded that the ghostly dog would walk through walls, although there was little mention of this spectre being of a malevolent nature. This is supported by an extraordinary sighting of the phantom hound, involving a family member who one day, whilst perched on a seat in the bay window in one of the main rooms upstairs (the Queen's Room), over-looking the moat, became aware of a strange dog which appeared on the other side of the room. The woman was not scared by the presence of the creature and, if anything, became endeared by it. She decided she would approach the dog, moving slowly away from the bay window. As she neared the animal it suddenly vanished into thin air. However, the area she had been sitting in began to creak and in one mighty yawn the entire bay window crumbled and plummeted to the moat below. Had the spectral dog saved her life?

The story was related to writer James Wentworth-Day, and the legend of this encounter has embedded itself into the folklore of Leeds. However, there is an alternative ghost story connected to the window which overlooks the moat, and oddly this one is without mention of a phantom dog. On the bay window a General Martin of Gibraltar was said to snooze, but one night his two sisters had a terrible dream in which they saw the wall outside crumble. They were so convinced that their dream would come true that the next day the two women removed the mattress from the sill. When the night drew in, and General Martin chose to sleep elsewhere, the bay window did indeed collapse and plummet to the waters below.

Maybe the legend of the ghostly black dog was nothing more than a sinister creation added to the original, less dramatic tale, to beef it up. Even so, the alleged spectral hound, whatever its truth, appears to have some ghostly friends.

More recent sightings of a large, dark-coloured dog, and also a small, white terrier-type dog (said to scratch at several of the doors throughout the castle) could be explained by two pictures which sit on the wall in the Upper Bridge Corridor. A photo of a large hound, and a sketch of a terrier (drawn by Alejo Vidal-Quadras in 1971), are proof that Lady Baillie owned such animals – the terrier was named Smudge, the Great Dane named Danny (Lady Baillie also owned another

'Smudge' –
does this small, white terrier
still haunt the castle?

Could the spirit of one of Lady Baillie's deceased pet dogs be responsible for the
modern legend of the Hellhound?

Great Dane called Boots), so maybe these two friendly dogs still frequent the castle. The Great Dane, if seen in ghostly form today, could possibly melt into the fearsome legend of the Hellhound many years ago. Mind you, it's also worth noting that the castle grounds harbour a dog-collar museum.

Leeds Castle is said to also be haunted by an unknown female spectre. Adorned in a long, flowing dress and always brushing her hair, her ghostly form is seen gliding throughout the grounds of the castle and also in the Queen's Room. There appears to be no origin to the ghost story, although some have surmised that the spectral woman was once married to an old Lord Fairfax. Legend has it that as soon as they were married, the bridegroom was immediately filled with deep regret, and calmly murdered his new wife and then carried on with her sister! In their *Encyclopaedia of Ghosts & Spirits*, John and Anne Spencer give a different take on the ghostly legend, sourcing Alice Pollock's *Portrait of my Victorian Youth*, they state:

Psychometrist Miss Alice Pollock was experimenting on one of the rooms at Leeds Castle in Kent known as Henry VIII's room, by touching objects in an attempt to experience events from another time. Miss Pollock was a relative of the family living at Leeds Castle; the relative chose this room as it was the one Alice Pollock's own parents had used when they stayed there.

After a period of receiving no impressions whatsoever, the room suddenly changed, losing its comfortable modern appearance and becoming cold and bare and carpetless. Logs were burning in the fireplace which was now in a different position. A tall woman in a white dress, deep in concentration and greatly anguished, was walking up and down the room. A history of the castle suggests that the room had been the prison of Queen Joan of Navarre, Henry V's stepmother, who had been accused of witchcraft by her husband.

61

Shadows around Leeds

Leeds Village harbours a George Lane, which houses The George Inn pub. The public house was built around 1652, and the surrounding fields and lanes were said to house the Augustinian Priory, said to date back to 1119. It was closed down in 1539 by Henry VIII, and then became a house, which was knocked down in the late eighteenth century. Although nothing remains of the original settlements, there have long been reports of spectral monks peacefully gliding through the woods and fields which now thrive here. Monks are common in ghost folklore, but recent sightings seem scarce to say the least.

Apparition at Abbey Farm

This small building was said to have had strong connections to the Leeds Priory and was once described as a 'white-faced homestead'.

In 1908, Writer Charles Igglesden, in the eighth volume of *A Saunter Through Kent With Pen And Pencil*, under the Leeds section, wrote of several ghost stories told to him by an old friend named George Gibbons, who as a boy had numerous encounters. In reference to Gibbons, Igglesden wrote:

He Said: 'Many are the ghost stories I have heard – one, I well remember, told me by the waggoner, old Dapper Foreman. He said that more than once when he has gone to bait his horses at four o'clock in the morning he found the animals all in a sweat and trembling with fright and their manes and tails tied up in little knots. I can scarcely believe it and yet I cannot entirely disbelieve it after what I have seen myself in the old fields – and in broad daylight too. I was sixteen-years old and at four o' clock on a summer's afternoon saw a ghost near the Abbey pond. It turned into four different figures; then it ran to the farther end of the Abbey farm on the east side of the Upper Street; next it took a course through the hedge and fruit grounds of the late Edward Gibbons my cousin, towards the back part of the Old Manor House and Viney's pond, and then – was seen no more. I was not dreaming, I was wide awake. It was a mystery I have never been able to explain away.'

LENHAM

Lenham appears in the book of Domesday as Lerham and Lertham. It takes its name from the stream which rises within it.

Another Quaker Ghost?

If the case of the Bearsted Quaker-type figure spooked you, then you may be slightly more warmed by the following ghost story, albeit concerning a similar type of figure.

A Joanna Robinson was living with her parents, who owned the Lurcock's grocery store in The Square at Lenham. The building dates back to 1480; its creaking beams a testament to its longevity. During the 1800s, it was owned by the Lurcock family who, since 1821, ran a grocery from the building.

Joanna's story began one afternoon in 1975 when she was feeling unwell with tonsillitis and was unable to attend school. Her father, Tony, was in the garden. Suddenly she heard the brass handle of the room she was in rattle and she was aware of a presence. She was in bed and dismissed it, thinking that maybe one of the staff had entered; until she saw the man. He was dressed in a Quaker-type tall hat and black cloak.

The feet of the character appeared to be in the ground – this type of anomaly is often reported in ghost sightings and could suggest that the figure is still in its own time when the floor of the building may have been lower. This could also explain some sightings of ghosts without heads or seemingly floating on air.

Joanna was not alarmed by the spectre, and the family believed he made his presence known to assure Joanna she would recover. Although Joanna never saw the ghostly man again, the family noticed their dog Fifi would be seen staring upstairs at an unseen presence.

A woman named Joan Walls backed up the claims of the Robinson family when she reported that twenty-five years earlier she'd worked in the area as a hairdresser. She commented:

> One day I was bending down, putting on some slippers, when I pulled a muscle really bad in my back. It was so painful I couldn't work. We had a couple who used to visit and he was a medium and healer. He told me I had been working too hard and I would now have to take it easy

because of the injury. He said, 'The Quaker thinks you're doing too much as well. He says you must slow down. I was a bit taken aback. 'Who are you talking about?' I said, and he said, 'Didn't you know about him? He's here now, standing by your bed!'

Although Joan never saw the Quaker figure, she would often report that her cat would act strange and stare as if someone had walked by. A young woman Joan met a couple of years later also mentioned seeing the figure.

The Red Lion

It is no surprise that old public houses appear in books about ghosts. The pub is situated in The Square, an area granted its first Market Charter in 1206 by King John. The Red Lion in Lenham is haunted by an old man who was once said to have rested at the pub whilst on a pilgrimage to Canterbury.

The Red Lion, Lenham.

The Harrow Inn, on Warren Street.

The Harrow Inn

This wonderful inn is situated not far from Lenham on Warren Street. It dates back to the seventeenth century and was once an ideal stop-over for travellers en route to Canterbury in east Kent.

A young female spirit has been felt by researchers who have conducted investigations into the haunting of the pub. It is alleged that the woman had a terrible accident in a neighbouring field and was laid to rest at the inn. In the cellar of the property a strong male presence has been sensed. In one of the upstairs rooms there is said to loiter the ghost of a young boy aged around twelve years old.

Investigations from ghost hunting groups and psychics have produced photographs of orbs, which are always debatable, considering such forms were never recorded in ghostly activity before the invention of digital cameras. Some researchers believe that orbs represent the beginning of a spirit form, but sceptics argue that such orbs are nothing more than specks of dust, picked up by the camera which the naked eye cannot see.

Chills at Chilston Park Hotel

In 1997, as reported by author Andrew Green, a Claire Tierney – a member of staff that caters for the comfort of guests at the hotel – saw a ghost. As she was walking up the staircase of the eighteenth-century manor house she noticed the reflection of a figure in eighteenth-century dress. This was no shock to Claire, as several members of staff were known, on occasion, to be dressed in such attire. However, when Claire turned to greet the man, who was wearing full footman's livery, the figure had completely

Chilston Park Hotel.

vanished. Even more bizarre, when Claire then looked back at the mirror, the ghostly reflection was visible once again. According to Claire another member of staff had heard about the apparition, which had apparently been seen on a number of occasions.

LINTON

Linton is a very small village, whose name possibly derives from the Anglo-Saxon 'lilian tun' – the lily growing settlement. It was first recorded in the twelfth century as Lilintuna.

The Bull Inn
Built in the fifteenth century, The Bull Inn sits in a large building which used to exist as three separate businesses – a post office, a barbers and a pub. When it first began life as a public house, there was rumour that admittance was reserved solely for men, and women were not permitted to enter. However, one of the spirits said to frequent the pub is a female adorned in a black dress with dark hair tied up in a bun. A gentleman was sensed in the top bar by Steve, a medium who runs the Ghost Search UK website. Several other spirits were contacted during an investigation in 2007, but whether any of these apparitions were connected to the pub, or more so to the individuals attempting to communicate with them, is unknown.

The pub is also said to be haunted by a domestic cat, and some of the unseen ghosts are said to call out the names of certain customers.

All Saints' Church, Loose.

The Weird Well

One peculiar and obscure anecdote in reference to Linton comes from an area which was once known as Goosewell Lane. At this location it was said there was a covered well which had supernatural properties. It was believed to have restorative qualities; those who were ill and who drank from it were miraculously cured. The water hole would become known as the 'ghost well' and then 'goose well'. Another legend states that a witch used to live within the vicinity of the well. She was known to sell minced mice and dried rats' tails. However, the locals opposed to her dwelling too near to the well and so drove her out, for fear of her contaminating the water.

Loose

Loose Valley is a picturesque setting for a quaint ghost story. It is situated 3 miles south of Maidstone. The village has Saxon roots and is recognisable for its tranquil stream which winds through the valley. Malcolm John once wrote, 'Loose village is no place for the car, and to be appreciated, should be visited on a crisp winter morning, when a walk along the stream is enchanting and culminates in a visit to the Old Wool House, a heavily-timbered National Trust property.'

A Loose Legend

The evangelical All Saints' Church, which has no record of being built, although it is believed that a church sat on the site in Saxon times, harbours a rather spooky story. Roger Thornburgh, in his 1978 book *Exploring Loose Village*, writes:

> On the south side of the church tower there are two old table tombs, memorials to the Crispe and Penfold families who occupied Old Loose Court for many years. Just behind is a pillar memorial to the Charlton family of Pimps Court along Bushbridge Road. Its top is curved with three hideous faces, intended, so it is suggested, to frighten away the Devil.
>
> Tradition has it that if you stick a pin in the yew tree, run around it anti-clockwise twelve times (at midnight some say) and

look in the small tower window above the Charlton memorial, you will see a face. Younger villagers add that what is seen is the missing fourth face from the top of the pillar. An older and much more macabre version of the story is that having stuck a pin into the tree and run around it twenty-four times, you stand on the table near the porch, look through the little trefoil window and see a woman killing a baby. These fragments of folklore seem to be as near as we in Loose can come to having a resident ghost.

Stick Man!

Some ghost stories, if believed, could be explained as recordings of past events – i.e. a phantom coach and horses still travelling its old route, a monk gliding in an area where an old Priory used to sit – but some ghost stories are completely baffling, and even comical in their surreal nature.

On the 14 January 2003, a chap named Simon posted a bizarre story on the forum of *Fortean Times* magazine (the magazine has, since the 1970s, covered stories of strange phenomena). He revealed:

The following account is slightly short-ened but otherwise unchanged and comes from my diary record for Tuesday, 31 October 1978. Only the names have been changed. We were all aged between fifteen and seventeen at the time. The Loose Valley referred to is near Maidstone in Kent. My diary record also indicates that there was a new moon on that night:

'I will record a rather unpleasant experience which took place tonight. A group of about ten of us were sitting chatting in the Loose Valley at about midnight. After about forty-five minutes Will leapt to his feet slapping his head saying there was a bee in his hair; he looked absolutely terri-fied. Both Dorothy and I saw the outline of a tall, thin figure wearing a hat danc-ing behind him. Will said later it was as if a terrifically loud buzzing was coming up through the top of his head. However only Rachel heard any buzzing.

We partially satisfied ourselves that it must have been a bees' nest, and so we moved a little distance away. As we moved away Dorothy and I saw a ring outlined in the grass which enclosed where we had been sitting. Eventually it started raining so we headed for Rachel's house. As we left I turned around and saw the same thin black figure walk across the opening between the trees to where we had been sitting.

We had been sitting in Rachel's bed-room for a while, when I looked at Will who was reading and saw an amorphous black blob drop out of his hair onto the bed. I was the only one who saw this. A few seconds later a black shape started whizzing around. The main movement was from bottom left to top right as I was

A weird apparition known as Stick Man haunts Loose village.

sitting, getting larger during the movement and inducing a great fright. About four people altogether saw this.

Later the girls slept in a room together. Apparently Rachel and Molly saw the black blob in the curtains during the night. I, however, had an excellent night's sleep. On first awakening I saw the thin black figure silhouetted against the wardrobe doors. I must admit I lost my calm last night and was bloody terrified by the whole thing.'

I have now moved away from the South East, but I occasionally meet Will. Even twenty years later he has been extremely unwilling to discuss the events of that night in any detail as he still found the memory disturbing. During our last meeting I gained a little more of his account. He was not aware of the thin figure which I saw behind him during the initial buzzing. Unprompted by me he did recall the black blob falling out of his hair, which I thought I alone witnessed. However, he recalls it dropping onto the pages of the book he was reading rather than onto the bed as I recalled. Will also recalls more of the girls' account of their night after retiring. Apparently the blob had several times appeared near the curtains and moved, while silhouetted against a bright light which appeared to come from outside but did not correspond to any street lamp or likely car lights.

This has been the only 'supernatural' experience of my life.

Banks wine bar, at Bank Street.

Maidstone Central

Banks Wine Bar

Bank Street is said to be one of, if not *the* oldest street in Maidstone. At No. 76 sits Banks wine bar. This suave bar is nestled just off the High Street and is rumoured to be so haunted that the Most Haunted investigative team were interested in conducting a vigil there.

At the back of the premises the old Victorian baker's ovens can still be viewed, and it's at the

rear of Banks that the ghost has been seen and felt the most. A monk in black robes is said to tamper with the electrics of the building, and for at least nine years staff have been spooked by the figure. The building is said to date back 500 years, so maybe this monk is simply a recorded spirit; but evidence suggests otherwise. When the *Most Haunted* team were keen to investigate, the bar owner and staff were reluctant and so decided to ask the spirit for a sign as to whether they should proceed.

One evening, five members of staff attempted to communicate with the monk. They told him that if he wished no filming to take place then he should give a sign. With that came a terrible thump from upstairs, and when the noise was investigated the manager found a large shattered mirror on the floor. Also, on another occasion, voices were heard upstairs by staff and when they went to investigate they discovered that the television had been turned on. In the past, glasses have been seen to fly across the room, and this seems a common occurrence in many haunted pubs and bars.

Despite the strange activity, the manager of Banks wine bar feels that the spirit is friendly, and only gets upset when there is upheaval or intrusion. This seems to be a fair reaction from the monk, considering that this particular entity has resided in this building a lot longer than the staff, probably by a few hundred years!

The Bower Inn

Situated at No.66 Tonbridge Road, The Bower Inn appears to be an extremely haunted public house. Lisa Baker, who runs the pub, mentioned that the area of land, that the building sits on, was purchased in 1654 (known once as Bower, which consisted of some 275 acres – in the same area there exists a Bower Place, Bower Mount Road, Bower Lane and a Bower Street). There are records of the building existing as far back as 1801, and in 1851 five families were said to reside at the premises. The resident ghost is called Sidney, but whether it's him who keeps turning the Guinness off we'll never know. Activity is sporadic, despite the mentions of a male ghost sighted standing in the corner of a room, and the fact that one barmaid refuses to enter the cellar on her own. One chap, named Roy, commented that whilst in the cellar one day a horrendous cold feeling enveloped his body.

The Bower Inn – the haunt of Sidney.

The Coopers Cask

At No.50 Bower Lane sits The Coopers Cask. This pub has a vague ghost story. It is rumoured that an old lady sporting bygone fashions has been seen in the vicinity of the women's toilets.

The Dog & Gun

This friendly public house is situated at No.213 on the Boxley Road out of Maidstone. It was once rumoured that a tunnel beneath the pub served Maidstone prison, and that prisoners were transported via this secret passage. Executions which took place at Penenden Heath involved carts full of criminals passing by the pub en route to their death. It is said that an old woman haunts the pub, particularly in the area of the stairs which lead to the attic – attic areas always seem to feature heavily in spooky stories! A landlady and her son have reported, on a few occasions, that they've stumbled down the stairs as if someone has pushed them from behind. Again, invisible assailants often seem intent on causing mischief, although not always to cause harm but simply to startle witnesses. It is possible that the ghostly old lady once resided at the pub; maybe she herself took a tumble down the stairs.

The Eagle Inn

The only strange activity reported from this pub, at No.56 Brewer Street, is the mysterious turning off of the gas.

The First & Last

This pub can be found at No.40 Bower Place; the ghost of a small child has been felt here in the past.

Fishermans Arms

At No.40 Lower Stone Street is the Fishermans Arms, said to be one of the oldest buildings in Maidstone. Although listed in the 1700s as a beer retailer, the building dates back to the 1430s. The resident ghost may date back to the Civil War (seventeenth century) and his name is 'Black Jack'. When the building used to be a farm shop, albeit one which sold ale, it was said that 'Black Jack' – possibly

The Dog & Gun is haunted by an old lady.

a Roundhead (members of the Parliamentary in opposition to the Cavaliers) – was shot and stumbled into the building where he died. Modern reports of the darkly-clad figure seem scant, but an ex-landlady did report seeing a figure in black, and that's where the figure got its sinister name.

The Green Room

This cool lounge bar used to sit at No.70 Bank Street in the town, and was formerly Project Blue and before that Café Rouge. It ceased trading in September 2009. A former member of staff reported that the building was haunted by the ghost of a little girl and that, whilst working there, she once felt a presence press on her arm. People in the cellar have reported the sound of footsteps up ahead in the main bar and the sound like a child skipping. The cellar area has spooked many staff; it is rumoured that tunnels used to run from under the bar and that the local monks used to meet in the dank passageways, although such tunnels have long since been bricked up.

The Greyhound

This building, once situated on Wheeler Street, was said to have been over 270 years old, and was eventually demolished to make way for a new housing estate.

Legend has it that a cavalier haunted the premises when it existed as The Greyhound public house. Several spirits made themselves known to a group of investigators in 2009, but most of these appear as vague entities not connected with the pub.

The Hazlitt Theatre

Built in 1869, the Hazlitt Theatre was constructed originally as a concert hall, with the use of stone columns taken from the old market site. The theatre was renamed in 1955 after William Hazlitt, born in 1778, who founded it; it sits on Earl Street in the town centre.

Despite a handful of ghost hunts over the years, and the claims that some spiritualist mediums have picked up different entities, most investigations have drawn a complete blank at the theatre. In November 2010, the manager of the theatre stated that the only ghostly rumour concerns a woman in a type

The Hazlitt Theatre.

This building used to house The Green Room, haunted by a little girl.

of maid outfit, who is said to roam the balcony area. Oddly, the balcony is relatively new, dating back to the 1900s.

Holy Trinity Church

During the 1970s, a Lesley Bridger was taking an afternoon stroll in the graveyard with her dog when she saw three women dressed in Victorian attire, and wearing large-brimmed bonnets, hovering over the ground. Instead of being terrified by the women, Lesley decided to investigate further and approached the figures, but they disappeared near the location of a flat stone which had been set in the ground. Bizarrely, the inscription mentioned that three women, all daughters of the vicar, had died within a few days of each other of scarlet fever.

Lesley also heard about other people who had seen the ghostly trio in the vicinity of the churchyard.

Maidstone Museum

Maidstone Museum & Art Gallery can be found on St Faiths Street in the town centre. It was formerly the aptly named Chillington Manor, an Elizabethan building constructed in 1562; the museum being established in 1858. The Great Hall and Withdrawing Room within the building date back to the original construction, whilst the Cloisters and Long Gallery remain from a Tudor building. At the rear of the Elizabethan building a large wing was added in 1698 and work continued until 1743. The East Wing was added in 1869 (extended in 1889) and now holds the Bentlif Art Gallery. The West Wing was constructed in 1873, while the Victoria Gallery, which harbours the library, was built between 1897 and 1899.

Ghost hunter Frederick Sanders visited an area of the museum, known in 1935 as the Baxter Room, and despite being initially impressed with the building and its airy atmosphere, suddenly became overwhelmed

Maidstone Museum & Art Gallery.

by a feeling of sadness. Frederick noted that his eyes welled up with tears and so he left the building, unable to contain his emotion. In 1937 Frederick returned but could not find such a room, and the following year visited again with the same result. However, in 1940, when his interest in ghostly phenomena took hold, Sanders once again visited the museum and found the room. Although Sanders could find no stories of ghosts for the room, at 2.00 p.m. one afternoon Sanders decided to browse over the pictures. After a couple of hours he once again became overwhelmed with emotion, which he believed was connected to a print named 'The Belle of the Village'. Tears filled his eyes every time he concentrated on the old print, and when he walked away the sorrow would cease, but when he returned his gaze to the picture, again the depression smothered him. It has also been claimed that Sanders, and others

who have been in the presence of it, have sensed a ghostly presence from a picture called 'Flora the Gypsy Girl'.

The picture is currently housed at the entrance to the museum, and under it is mentioned the experience Frederick Sanders had.

In the May of 1998, ghost hunter Andrew Green spoke to Veronica Tonge, keeper of the Fine Art Collection, who stated that no-one had ever reported anything supernatural. The closest anyone came to any kind of paranormal activity was the sense of an unusual vibe emanating from the gypsy girl painting.

Researcher Kevin Payne recalled that during his early teens he heard a story on the local radio that a security guard at the museum had tried to set fire to the property because it had been haunted by the ghost of an Egyptian princess. The guard was believed to be insane and yet, shortly after, it was rumoured that another member of staff had attempted the

One of the first ghost hunt's at Maidstone Museum & Art Gallery was conducted in the late 1930s by Frederick Sanders.

The painting titled 'Flora the Gypsy Girl' is said to emit unusual vibes.

'It's not as scary as that', she said. 'It will be brilliant if we can catch something on camera'.

The investigation team held a séance and used an Ouija board. Two members of the team claim they were touched by a little girl. Mrs Vickers also claimed to have sensed the presence of a little boy who was perched on a ladder in the library. The *KM Extra* of October 7 stated that the team, whilst on the Ouija board, contacted five spirits, including William Hazlitt who died in 1830.

On the 28 October 2005, the *Kent Messenger* newspaper ran a story on several Maidstone-related ghost investigations conducted by the Southern Paranormal Investigation Team. The story stated:

same act, driven by some unseen force. There are also rumours that a fellow in Elizabethan clothes has been seen in the museum, and also a little girl from the same period.

The *Kent Messenger* of 25 September reported that a group of ghost hunters were going to investigate the museum.

A 14-strong group of enthusiasts are hoping to experience some unexplained events, such as apparitions and disembodied voices. The spirit of a gypsy girl is said to haunt the museum and both staff and visitors have reported strange experiences when visiting the 'gypsy girl' painting in the museum's Baxter Room.

Although the visit by the group follows a filming session by TV Medium Derek Acorah, Corriene Vickers, one of the investigative team's founding members, said programmes such as his *Most Haunted* series gave paranormal investigations a bad name.

In the last month the group had had hair-raising experiences in both the Maidstone Museum and Bentlif Art Gallery…Mrs Vickers and two members of the group were touched by a spirit child during a recent visit to Maidstone Museum, but she cast doubt on the theory that one of the art gallery's paintings is haunted. She said: 'We didn't feel anything at all from the painting or in that room. But there are definitely places in there that have spirit activity. We sense it as soon as we walk in – The Cloisters being one.'

Maidstone Town Hall

Built in 1763, the Town Hall, situated on the High Street, is a Georgian building which used to act as the Magistrates' Court; it is said to be haunted by a judge. The ghostly activity appears to be at a minimum, but one member of staff reported that in 2009 a psychic was called in and a nightly vigil was conducted. The psychic commented that a judge may have been responsible for the sound of footsteps on the stairs. The build-

Maidstone Town Hall is supposedly haunted by a judge.

ing used to house an eighteenth-century prison, which sat above the council chamber. An open market used to be held at the front, until it was built upon and became part of the Town Hall.

Mote Park

Mote Park, accessible off Mote Avenue, is one of the largest public parks in the south of England. It covers more than 250 acres and harbours a 30 acre lake. The park dates back to the Middle Ages.

A Ghostly Encounter

On 18 September 2010, a woman named Marian from Maidstone posted the following ghost story, in relation to Mote Park, on the *Daily Mail* website:

> I took the dogs to Mote Park one morning a few years ago, and as I parked the car at the top end of the Park, I saw another

car coming along to take its place beside mine. I got out of the car to get the dogs out, and glanced at the other car. In the backseat sat two old ladies, one with white curly hair and wearing glasses, the other with short darker grey hair. One was leaning over the other, presumably looking for something in the big black handbag on her lap, closest to me. I didn't notice the driver at the time. Anyway I had two dogs to see to, so got them out and locked up the car. I looked at the next car again. A thin, sad-faced middle-aged

Mote Park harbours a lot of paranormal activity.

75

man left the driver's side with a ginger dog. But the ladies were no longer in the car. The man and his dog were the only souls I could see across the open grass, and no other cars were there. Weird or what?

The Haunted Family

During the 1970s, a couple moved into a new top-floor flat built in the area of Mote Park. This area may have once housed the old park gatehouse. After six months strange things began to happen. Items of clothing would go missing, such as jumpers put into a chest of drawers, but the next day were nowhere to be found. On one occasion the wife put her rings on top of the toilet cistern whilst cleaning the bathroom, but when she'd finished the jewellery was also nowhere to be found. A week later the missing rings were found … on the cistern, even though the couple had used the toilet time and time again.

When the couple settled into their home, their four-year-old niece would occasionally stay over on a weekend. She would sleep on a smaller bed next to the double bed of the couple. One morning, at around 3.00 a.m., the man awoke to see a girl, around the age of ten, standing and looking down at his niece. The witness described the girl as very clear but like a water colour painting. She had long, fair hair, was wearing a pale blue dress, and also wore a high-necked white blouse. Her garments reminded him of something from the 1800s.

The man told his wife about the encounter the following morning, to which she replied that he must have been dreaming. On another occasion, the man's wife was on her knees cleaning the kitchen floor when suddenly she looked up and could, see directly in front of her, a pair of black, shiny, button-up boots, approximately size 3. Above these were white stockings. The limbs vanished.

The atmospheric park in winter; a perfect setting for a ghost story … or two!

The couple never discussed the haunting with anyone else, at the time, as they felt that they would be ridiculed; however, three other people who knew them also saw the ghost of the young girl. These sightings took place over the next five years. The girl was always seen at night, standing by a bed and looking down on someone.

The couple claimed that they saw the girl once a year, usually near the festive period and the incidents where items went missing were reasonably frequent. The couple decided to call in a clergyman, who performed an exorcism of the flat, and one month later the girl was seen again. After being at the flat for eight years the couple moved out. They've never experienced anything since.

The male witness believed the girl had passed away at a young age and was of no harm. In fact, the couple felt some kind of rapport with her, to the extent that whenever they went away and left the property they would ask the ghostly presence to look after the flat.

The Muggleton Inn

If it's a pint and a pub lunch you're after, then The Muggleton Inn, at No.8-9 High Street, is for you. Muggleton was the word Charles Dickens used to describe Maidstone in his book *The Pickwick Papers*.

The building was constructed in 1827 and was used as the Kent Fire Brigade head office. Stretching over four grand floors, one of which (the boardroom) was described by the Earl of Romney as 'One of the best possessed by any company in Great Britain.'

When the fire brigade moved elsewhere, an insurance company took over the premises. As a pub, The Muggleton Inn has existed for just over a decade and has recently gone through an impressive refurbishment. Whether the resident ghosts are happy, we'll have to wait and see.

The Muggleton Inn, in the town centre.

Throughout the building staff have reported the feeling of being watched by an unquantifiable entity, while vague male energies have been reported in the cellar areas which stretch beneath the building.

Museum of Kent Life

Formerly Sandling Farm – which dated back to 1555 – the Museum of Kent Life, is said to be teeming with ghosts. Situated at Cobtree, Lock Lane, in Maidstone, the 20 acre site hosts a variety of events which cater for children and adults alike. The land was once part of Allington Castle, then owned by Sir Thomas Wyatt, lover of Anne Boleyn. In four centuries the site has gone through several transformations – once being a Tudor farmstead, and then remodelled during the Georgian era, and again in Victorian times by then owner George Brundle.

A Gaggle of Ghosts

Ten buildings sit at the site and each reputedly has a ghost. Some of the ghostly experiences are obviously more vague than others. Some of the most stirring legends concern the tragic accident in 1912, in which a young farmer's wife named Rebecca Alexander was killed by a cart. Ever since this event Rebecca has haunted the area as a mournful spirit, determined to find her new-born baby, which survived the accident. Another young lady is said to roam the area of the Oast House and the pond. The Oast House is also haunted by a character named 'Peg Leg Jack', who lost his leg after a dispute with a local farmer.

One of the buildings, a barn, is said to be cursed and it has often been connected to the old gypsy caravan which sits in the place. It is also alleged that many decades ago, a German pilot, whilst flying over the village, crashed his plane into the roof of the tea-room. Does the tormented spirit still lurk in the shadows?

Visitors to the museum have often reported fleeting shadows, strange bumps in the night and on one occasion, in one of the windows, when the museum was closed for the night, a flickering candle had been observed.

Ghost Hunt-a-Go-Go

In 2008 *Your Maidstone* reported that a ghost hunt would take place at the Museum of Kent Life:

> … after the museum had teamed up with an event's company called Fright Nights for its Halloween '…gathering of ghosts' event, where a handpicked team of qualified clairvoyants, psychics and mediums will be giving visitors the chance to experience the site's haunted history and search for its ghostly residents.
>
> The event on 2 May, between 9 p.m. and 5 a.m., is the first ever overnight ghost hunt to be held at the farm museum.
>
> Museum director John Jordan said: 'We're well known throughout the country for our haunted happenings and are regularly approached by paranormal investigators who want to find out more. Teaming up with Fright Nights is a natural choice, they are the UK's leading ghost hunting specialists and have impressed us with their reputation for scientific accuracy and ability to deliver an unparalleled paranormal experience.'
>
> Fright Nights director Martin Jeffery said: 'We are delighted to be working exclusively with the famously haunted Museum of Kent Life and to be welcoming the public to our event so they can discover the museum's haunted history for themselves.'

This wouldn't be the last time the organisers teamed up to explore the spooky side of the area.

The Oast House at the Museum of Kent Life is haunted by several spooks.

Two months before a group of investigators visited the place, one of the visitors in the vicinity of the Oast House reported the presence of several Civil War soldiers. One of the men, the main presence, was dressed in a lobster-tail helmet and wore brown clothes. Another ghostly figure was said to have lead his horse by the reigns. The psychic also commented that the soldiers appeared to be exhausted, as if they had been in a battle, and dated their uniform to 1646. Further research revealed that she was only two years out and that the battle had taken place two years later.

In the gardens it was noted that a man named Jackson was present. Dressed in a flat cap, the spirit told the investigator he used to be a gardener and died at the age of eighty-four. One of the more bizarre ghosts reported during the investigation concerned a white donkey painted with stripes and a blue colour. It was confirmed that a donkey did in fact reside in the area many years ago and had been painted to make it look like a zebra!

A man in a wide-brimmed hat, and carrying a hay fork, had also been recorded, as well as a man named Wilson. The investigator also commented:

We moved from the small room area to the small circular room situated to the top of the Oast House. I soon became aware of the energy of a man from around 1196-1206. He was attired in armour, which included a white tabard with an ornate red cross; it had curved edges to it instead of the Christian cross of today. There was a loud sound from the downstairs as well as the build-up of a visible mist towards the entrance into the room. The name of De Courtney was mentioned; he wore a metal helmet, and chinked mail over his head and shoulders. I was told this man was of a monastic order, which led me to believe this man to have possibly been a Knights Templar. I then heard a phrase in Latin which sounded similar to '*et too ay fractum*' as well as the name of Sir Neville Croxley. There was the spirit of a second man who I perceived by the entrance into the room. He was a tall man and barrel-chested and was also attired in a military uniform. He sported a full beard, dark brown hair, with rounded facial features and was around 16 stones in weight. He told me that he carried a hand and a half sword and shield. He too wore a large white tabard. He mentioned the name of Simon De Courtney and then mentioned what sounded like 'Roux'.

Without a shadow of a doubt, I believe that several ghosts haunt the site which now harbours the Museum of Kent Life. It's no wonder that ghost hunts, particularly around Halloween, continue to this day.

A Bad (Smelling) Omen?

A bizarre haunting occurs on this estate in the form of putrid odours coming from the drains. Whilst many people may feel that smelly drains are normal, in this particular area the network of sewers beneath the place only begin to reek when a local resident dies!

Penenden Heath

This suburb in the town of Maidstone has a lot of dark history. During the Middle Ages the heath (now a recreation ground) was used for assemblies and many folk used to gather here. Such meetings, known as Shire Moots, were recorded in the Domesday

Penenden Heath. Public hangings used to take place here.

Book, where Penenden Heath was mentioned as Pinnedenna. The first recorded trial in English history took place on Penenden Heath in 1076, and involved Archbishop Lanfranc and Odo, Bishop of Bayeux.

The area took on a more macabre mood when people used to gather at the gallows to watch criminals being hanged for their crimes. It is commonly held that the name of Penenden derives from the Saxon pinian, meaning 'to punish'. Hangmen were said to have been on a wage of 11s 8d a year, although some executions were allegedly performed by the local ploughmen! The executions took place from the Anglo-Saxon period through to the nineteenth century, and between the twelfth and seventeenth centuries witches were executed on the heath.

A record from 1652 states:

Anne Ashby, alias Cobler, Anne Martin, Mary Browne, Anne Wilson, and Mildred Wright of Cranbrook, and Mary Read of Lenham, being legally convicted, were according to the Laws of this Nation, adjudged to be hanged, at the common place of Execution. Some there were that wished rather, they might be burnt to ashes; alledging that it was received opinion among many, that the body of a witch being burnt, her bloud is prevented thereby from becoming hereditary to her Progeny in the same evil.

The Maidstone Official Charter Brochure 1549-1949, compiled by Raymond Hewett, mentions the trial:

Trial of witches at the Assizes – According to a contemporary pamphlet, two of the accused confessed to the judge that they had been in communication with the devil. Anne Ashby of Cranbrook, one of the accused, 'fell into an extasie before the bench, and swell'd into a monstrous and vast bigness, screeching and crying out very dolefully; and being recovered, and demanded if the devil at that had possessed her. She replyed she knew not that, but she said that the Spirit Rug came out of her mouth like a mouse.'

In the March of 1678 it was noted that:

A woman is indicted for witchcraft at the Assizes – Prosecution witnesses said that she bewitched a young maid who had offended her. 'To make this pretence good there was produced a pint of blood full of nails and crooked pins bow'd into strange forms, all which the witnesses attested the maid had brought up by a vomit.'

On 22 July 1769, a Susannah Lott was convicted alongside Benjamin Buss for the poisoning of Lott's husband. Buss was executed. Lott was drawn to a hurdle on the Heath and hanged from a peg affixed to a stake. Her body was then shackled to the stake and after faggots had been piled around her, they were ignited and the body burnt to ash. Four years previous, highwayman Elias Shepherd (*see* Harrietsham segment) was hanged on Penenden Heath.

Many people, including alleged 'witches', were burned to death at Penenden Heath. (Illustration by Simon Wyatt)

The last public hanging at Penenden Heath was in 1830. A John Dyke, from Bearsted, was executed for burning a rick, although he was later proven innocent of the crime. It was also rumoured that some locals felt the heath had become too fashionable to stage such executions. Farmers complained that gathering crowds would trample their crops en route to the hangings.

Nowadays, football and cricket teams regularly play matches on the grass where so much death took place. The heath was home to a cricket club between 1786 and 1819. The Bull public house sits next to the green.

The Old Man

During the 1970s, a man was metal-detecting, illegally, on the heath. It was late when he felt a peculiar presence and that uncanny feeling as if being watched. Upon looking up towards the tree line (the trees in the area are said to date back centuries – there was once a myth that some criminals were hung from these instead of the gallows!) he observed a man in dark clothing standing by a wrought-iron fence which bordered the heath. The man was not perturbed by the figure and continued his search. Every minute or so the man scouring the ground would look up and see the figure staring back at him. He slowly

neared the figure and noticed it was an old man, but again, the witness was more interested in finding something of worth beneath the soil. Finally, the witness decided to approach the man and speak to him, but as he got to within a few metres the old man turned and walked straight through the fence and disappeared!

Any number of ancient spirits could haunt Penenden Heath. There is no doubt that there are many untold ghost stories pertaining to the stretch of land where death was a regular occurrence.

The Queen Anne pub.

The Queen Anne

Described as Maidstone's 'only gay pub', and situated at No.11 Queen Anne Road, the Queen Anne is rumoured to be haunted by a woman. Many years ago a road was situated where the front of the public house now sits, and it was here that a woman was killed after being run over by a cart. Staff have reported glasses falling off the shelves and there have been sporadic reports of a female figure walking in through the front door but vanishing. Whether or not this is the woman who died under the cart, we'll never know.

Royal Star Arcade

Formerly the Royal Star Hotel, this mini-shopping centre is said to be haunted by the ghost of a caretaker, who, during the 1970s, was observed by two families. A man in a flat cap and overalls was seen standing by one family member, who, at the time, when told by other witnesses, stated categorically they hadn't seen the man.

Sir Thomas Wyatt

This Beefeater restaurant and pub is located on the London Road. The ghost is said to be of a young woman, but details seem scant, although some ex-employees claimed to have seen her.

Undisclosed Location

Renowned ghost hunter Elliot O' Donnell, in his fascinating book *Confessions of a Ghost Hunter*, wrote, 'One of my most recent uncanny experiences was in the avenue of a private house near Maidstone.'

The house has a history. About 1812 the owner of it went on a visit to some friends, leaving two women servants in the house to look after it. Fearing burglars and thinking to outwit them, supposing they did break in, the two women hid all the silver in the house in the kitchen oven. However, one of them, in a fit of absent-mindedness, lit the kitchen fire, and the silver of course was very badly damaged. They were then, it seems, so fearful of the consequences (for servants, in those days, were not treated as considerately as they are now) that they drowned themselves in a lake in the grounds. Afterwards, a beautiful avenue leading to this lake acquired the reputation for being haunted, and it has been so reputed ever since.

A few years ago, a lady visitor at the house was found lying in a dead faint. On recovering consciousness, she told a strange tale. She said that, as she was walking up the avenue, she suddenly saw a woman approach her, clad in a very old-fashioned dress and wearing a kind of mob-cap. As they drew nearer to one another, the visitor saw the woman's face very distinctly, and it was so altogether horrible that she fainted. After this, various people saw the same figure, always in the avenue but not always at the same time.

It sometimes appeared in broad daylight. A gentleman who saw it one afternoon preceding him up the avenue, and consequently with its back turned towards him, thought, at first, that it was merely some eccentrically clad member of the household. But later, when he heard about the haunting, of which he was entirely ignorant on the occasion referred to, he was convinced from the description that was given him of it, that he had, on the said occasion, actually seen the ghost.

After hearing of these ghostly tales, Mr O'Donnell conducted a nightly vigil in the avenue and grounds of the house. He reported that he found the atmosphere brooding and depressive. His apprehension doubled when he stood by the water where he sensed an unseen presence. Whatever lurked in the shadows of night gave off an air of malevolence. Elliot could stand the eeriness no longer and so staked out the avenue instead, but whilst walking to the area, and coming to a junction of pathways, he was startled by an unseen presence which, by sound, seemed to rush towards him. O'Donnell drew back away from whatever unseen thing approached, but this action did not prevent the presence from bumping into him, although Elliot could see no shape or form.

In her book *Night Side of Nature or Ghost and Ghost Seers*, author Catherine Crowe speaks of a reputedly haunted house on, '… the road betwixt [sic] Maidstone and Tunbridge', stating:

There was nothing dismal about it; it was neither large nor old; and it stood on the borders of a well frequented road; yet I was assured it had stood empty for years; and as long as I lived in that part of the country it never had an inhabitant, and I believe was finally pulled down; and all for no other reason than that it was haunted.

Vinters Valley

There is only one report of a ghost in this wooded area and it comes from 1 October 2003, when, at 11.45 p.m., a man out walking was shocked to see another man dressed in Victorian attire. The spectre had long blonde hair which was tied back, but the most shocking aspect of the ghoul was the fact that it had no face or legs and yet appeared to move in a puppet-like fashion. The startled witness also noted that where the man's chest should have been, there was simply a black hole. The grisly ghost cavorted along the pathway from left to right and disappeared through a fence.

West Kent General Hospital

This old hospital, founded during the eighteenth century, was once situated on Marsham Street, and had 160 beds … and a resident ghost!

Author and supernatural expert Andrew Green wrote of the hospital:

… [it] has an excellent reputation but also a crying ghost. The hospital…like many others, has been altered, modified and enlarged over the years so there is little likelihood of ever establishing the identity of the phantom woman who cries so pitifully in one of the wards. Although she has not been seen in living memory, her sobs have been heard on numerous occasions, the most recent being during the autumn of 1978 by Mr Day, a charge-

The White Rabbit, on the Sandling Road.

nurse on night duty. Like some of the other members of the staff he has often been puzzled and has spent some time trying to gain further information regarding the distressing sounds.

White Rabbit

This restaurant and hotel, described as a 'vintage inn', is situated on the Sandling Road. It is haunted by the ghost of a little girl who is said to loiter in the vicinity of Room 8. Some witnesses, whilst staying at the hotel, have heard a voice of a young girl calling for her cat. On occasion, the door to Room 8 has been seen opening and closing of its own accord, whilst the bar area of the hotel was often subject to the flickering of lights.

NETTLESTEAD

With a population of just over 800, the village and civil parish of Nettlestead is situated on the road south-west of Maidstone. In 1763, Nettlestead was battered so severely by a hailstorm that buildings and trees suffered horrendous damage.

A trio of Ghosts

There doesn't appear to be too many ghost stories from Nettlestead, but the one which

often does the rounds is of some note. Legend has it that a footpath leads from the village church towards the River Medway. Every year (in November, around the 11th) a phantom bridge appears here and the spectre of a cowled monk, accompanied by a bound and gagged woman, can be seen on it. The monk tosses the woman into the water as she screams; the depths stifling her wails as the scene fades from view. Little else seems to be known about this extraordinary haunting.

Charles Igglesden, in his Nettlestead coverage from the eleventh volume of *A Saunter Through Kent With Pen And Pencil*, adds a touch more atmosphere to the ghostly tale, commenting:

> When the railway was constructed the driver of a train was told the story. 'Tell me which night this pair of ghosts are expected,' he said with a laugh. 'Tomorrow at midnight,' was his friend's

The village of Nettlestead.

84

reply. 'That's just the time I'm due to pass the haunted spot,' said the driver, as he clapped his hands to his legs to keep them warm, while he puffed huge clouds of smoke from his mouth. At midnight the train went past Nettlestead and just as it reached the spot where the old avenue used to pass through there was a thud and a strange noise. The train went on, but several yards further on the driver stopped it. 'I can't go on, Bill,' he said to the stoker. 'It was the ghosts.' Bill looked into his mates pale face, his scared eyes standing out in the dim light. 'No, I don't think you're fit to drive,' he said meaningly. They walked back cautiously and by the side of the line found to their horror a small mass of flesh and bone – the mangled body of a goat. But Bill's friend was taken to an asylum. He had laid the Nettlestead ghost, but at the cost of his reason.

OTHAM

This village, situated 3 miles to the south-east of Maidstone is often confused with Offham at West Malling. The church at Otham dates back to the 1540s.

The

Orchard Spot

The Orchard Spot exists as a pub/restaurant and function rooms on Spot Lane in Otham. Parts of the building date back to the 1500s, while restaurant timbers are believed to date back to the period of the Vikings. Since 2005 it has been a family-run business and although little has been experienced recently, the owners are fully aware of the ghostly history. Many years ago a disabled woman was said to have died in a chair in one of the back rooms, but the ghost who was picked up by psychic medium Chris Sillitoe suggests a male presence on the stairs. Strange feelings have been recorded in some of the older parts of the building.

SUTTON VALENCE

In 1798 Edward Hasted wrote of:

Town Sutton, alias Sutton Valence … the next parish eastward from Chart Sutton. It has the name of Valence from that eminent family, who continued long owners of it, and is called Town Sutton from the largeness of the village or town of it, in comparison of those of the adjoining parishes of the same name.

The Orchard Spot, Otham.

The village harbours the remains of a twelfth-century castle, which, according to the English Heritage website, '…was owned by a succession of important medieval lords'.

The only surviving remnants of the castle being the stone keep.

The Queens Head

This public house, dating back to the fifteenth century, sits on the High Street and is said to be extremely haunted. A Medium named Steve Moyle, who runs the Ghost Search UK website, wrote in 2008, in promotion of a ghost hunt at the pub:

> Oh boy, what a place. Imagine how many rings are on a tree and that's how many layers of spiritual past we have to uncover. This building is highly active with a capital H and covers a large area. The attic is not a place you will find the Landlord, although you will find me and my group up there on the night!! I have been requested by Mr Williams (Landlord) not to reveal too much of the active spirit that reside here…yet he requests your company to discover just what could be discovered! To wet your appetite I will say that prisoners were once held here, where the original bar was once sighted is an eye opener and two active spirits have been seen by various reputable people, that's without Mr Williams own personal encounter with an unseen energy … interested ?

Several spirits were picked up by the investigative team, including a woman in a pale blue dress wearing a bonnet. Spirits have made themselves known in the cellar and a man in dark garments was said to haunt the attic. This apparition was said to have died in 1801 and was a coachman. Despite the amount of seemingly spiritual connections some investigators and those with mediumship qualities claim, sceptics argue that more proof is needed. However, it must be stated that some people are more susceptible to paranormal activity than others, and whilst it's easy to dismiss a person's alleged ability to attract a number of spirits, there is no denying that when researched, some details given by possible spirit entities are accurate. Whilst it is fair to say that more evidence is required as proof of the afterlife and ghosts in general, thousands of eyewitnesses offer the best evidence in their own personal encounters and communications with the spirit world.

Wondrous Works!

The title of this segment comes from an old English ballad found by writer Charles Igglesden, which, in its full title reads, 'Comfort to the Afflicted or The Wondrous Works of God shown to the Widow and the Fatherless'. This folk tale concerns a Mary Blake, from the parish of Town Sutton, who was left with four children and applied to the parish for relief. Igglesden writes that the:

> …churchwarden of the day raised his voice against relief being given and his colleagues refused to help her. Upon which the unfortunate widow went home, told her little ones to pray to God for bread and then locked herself in her room with the purpose of taking her life.

Suddenly, as Mary Blake was about to commit the desperate act, a figure in white appeared before her, and with rays of hope and words of faith wrenched her from her woe. The churchwarden who refused to aid Mary Blake was found dead in his bed, his head smashed in, blood and gore splattered over the walls.

The incident was written of in a 199 line verse, the last few lines speaking of the churchwarden's death:

To bed he went that very night,
But was struck dead ere morning light.
His head was dashed in pieces small,
His blood was sprinkled on the wall.
A sad and dismal sight to view;
This many know for to be true,
The overseers sent straightaway,
For this distressed family,
And gave her tender babes relief,
This put an end to all her grief

Some have commented that the vision experienced by the suicidal woman was that of an angel, or possibly a life-saving ghost.

TESTON

Teston is a rural village located on the A26 out of Maidstone. The River Medway runs through Teston and a medieval bridge allows access across.

Boo! At Barham Court

The beautiful Barham Court is used for weddings, parties and other events. This old building was once inhabited by Reginald Fitz Urse, who in 1170, at Canterbury Cathedral, murdered Sir Thomas Beckett. Author Edward Hasted, when visiting Barham Court some time in the eighteenth century, commented that it was the '…greatest ornament of this part of the county.'

Barham Court has been used as a military hospital, and in the past both Winston Churchill and Queen Mary stayed there.

Due to its history, it's no surprise that this building has several ghosts. One such spirit is said to be a John Miles who, in 1852, perished at the age of sixty-seven in a fire on the property. Several other male ghosts have

Barham Court.

been contacted in the building by several ghost investigation groups. In the basement, a woman named Jenny, who allegedly died in 1912, made herself known to members of the Ghost Search UK team. A fourteen-year old girl was also contacted, and a sergeant named Norman Swain, who died in 1915, was also said to have come forward.

THURNHAM

Thurnham is a picturesque village 3 miles north-east of Maidstone, and much of its 3,194 acres sit within the North Downs. The Pilgrims Way runs through the parish.

Castle Capers

At Thurnham there is a haunting which bears a slight similarity to the faceless ghost seen at Vinters Valley. In June 2003, a group of people were standing around a crackling fire near Thurnham Castle when a man, adorned in a blue and green tunic, and standing around 7ft in height, ran by waving his hands wildly. The figure had no face, short hair, and vanished after a few seconds.

The castle is a twelfth-century flint construction with 10ft high walls, although the west wall is no longer standing. A couple of members of the Ghost Connections team, whilst on a visit to the castle a few years ago ,claimed to have seen a dark shape moving in the bailey of the castle, which they agreed appeared to be similar to a large dog. They also claimed that a deep growl emanated from the undergrowth, although in the past the wooded areas of Thurnham have been prowled by a very large cat resembling a melanistic (dark-coated) leopard.

TOVIL

The village of Tovil was once known for its paper mill industry, which ran along the Loose Stream, but it ceased in the 1980s.

The Phantom Cat

A Sharon Ramsden emailed the following ghost story:

> We [Sharon and her family] moved from Headcorn to Tovil in 1978. We stayed there for thirteen years. I was fourteen, my brother was seventeen. We had a tabby/white cat called Lollypop. One night my mother and I were watching television with the light off at about 11.00 p.m. when a black cat trotted from the kitchen past us and through the front-room door towards the stairs. We looked upstairs thinking at first that it was Lolly but there was nothing there. It happened at least once a week, we all saw it at different times and just got used to it. The house was No.109 Coombe Road which has now been pulled down and rebuilt.

Phantom cats, along with dogs, are probably the most common spectral animals sighted and are usually thought to be the ghosts of deceased pets.

The Haunted Treacle Mine

The following ghostly tales can certainly be taken with a pinch of…treacle! According to Wikipedia:

> Treacle mining is the fictitious mining of treacle (similar to molasses) in a raw form similar to coal. The subject purports to be serious but is an attempt to test credulity. Thick black treacle makes the deception plausible. The topic has been a joke in British humour for a century. The

paper mills around Maidstone, in Kent, were known as the Tovil Treacle Mines by locals, after the area where one of the mills owned by Albert E. Reed was situated. The company helped the myth with a float in Maidstone carnival with a 'treacle mine' theme.

One suggested answer to the story in this area is a rumour that the paper industry was threatened during the Second World War because there was no imported timber. Fermentation of straw was tried, creating a sticky goo. There were attempts to make paper from rags in the nineteenth century and an early commercial success was achieved by Samuel Hook and his son, Charles Townsend Hook, using straw at Upper Tovil Mill in the 1850s. The road next to Upper Tovil Mill became known, and was later named, as Straw Mill Hill. To produce pulp, the straw was cooked in hot alkali. After separation of the fibre, the remaining liquid looked like black treacle. Upper Tovil Mill closed in the 1980s and the site was used for a housing estate.

The Strange Tales From The Doll's House blog mentions a couple of ghost stories from these mines. Whether such tales, or indeed mines, are purely fictitious is open to debate, it's up to you to decide. The first haunting is mentioned by a Stephen Piper, who comments, 'I live right on Bockingford (a hamlet neighbouring Tovil), you can still hear the ghost miners shuffling their pots at night… some say they still mine for the old liquid gold to this day, led by old "Sticky Widget", treacle foreman from hell.'

Another member of the rumour mill stated, 'I know of people who have seen the ghosts … sticky hair, bulbous noses, glazed skin and molasses-fever.'

The website owner also mentioned, with regards to Treacle Tower:

The top of the tower was sealed off in the 1950s after two local youths fell to their death whilst trying to get some 'treacle scrapings' from inside the rim of the tower. Some say the tower is haunted and that you can hear the lads' deathly wail if you press your ear firmly to the tower.

ULCOMBE

The village of Ulcombe is only populated by approximately 850 people. The claim to fame of the village is a yew tree situated in All Saint's Church which is said to be more than 3,000 years old!

A Phenomenon?

Ghost stories within Ulcombe are scarce, but one extraordinary phenomenon was recorded from 1985, when according to the Historic Kent website:

…volunteers working on a £100,000 restoration scheme at Ulcombe Church dug out hundreds of human bones, boars teeth, and other assorted relics from around the bottom of All Saint's Church's rag stone walls. At the moment the first shovel hit the first bone, a flash of lightning ripped across the sky and there was an exceptionally loud crash of thunder followed by heavy rain. In that instant, 2,000 years of Christian teaching fell away and betrayed lurking pagan apprehension among the diggers.

Nobody really knows how old the bones are, but it has been suggested that the church was probably built on a pre-Christian burial site and that the remains recalled those long-ago interments.

WATERINGBURY

The River Medway plays a major part in the history of Wateringbury. According to the Wateringbury Parish Council website, the village, '…is one of a chain of Upper Medway Valley villages … from Allington Lock, below Maidstone, to Tonbridge, the river is well used all summer by holiday cruisers and the riverside at Wateringbury is always lined with them.'

Magical Properties?

Above the Bow Bridge, the Wateringbury Stream meets the Medway, and in the vicinity of Pizien Well Road, at the west end of the parish, sits what is called a Holy Well. The name Pizen may have either derived from the local family name of Peizen, or could be a corruption of 'poison'. However, this appears to contradict the local legend, for it is said that many years ago the water had healing properties and other miraculous attributes. Newly weds would often visit the well because the water was said to ensure fertility. No-one is sure as to whether the well is still visited by the odd bride, eager to sip from the magic waters in the dead of night.

A Supernatural Storm?

For many centuries, bizarre storms, of seemingly supernatural force, have wreaked havoc throughout Kent. One such tempest raged through Wateringbury in the August of 1773. Strangely, the storm raged for only thirty or so minutes and the village was battered by hailstones which were so huge – measuring 10in in circumference – that for over a month after they remained piled up. Local wildlife scurried into shelter to seek refuge from this treacherous storm which badly damaged buildings and crops, and as thunder boomed across the sky and forks of lightning shot down from the black Heavens, it may have appeared to some as if all Hell had broken loose.

Pizien Well Road in Wateringbury is said to harbour a well boasting supernatural powers.

WEST FARLEIGH

The West Farleigh village website states that the village:

> …mentioned in the Doomsday Book, is situated 4 miles south west of the centre of Maidstone on the south side of the River Medway Valley. William Cobbett pronounced the Medway Valley west of Maidstone the finest in England and West Farleigh bears testimony to that opinion. The village remains traditionally agricultural, has an unspoilt Norman church, a Village Green with excellent views and some fine houses including Smiths Hall which has been the setting for several films.

The Haunting of Hill Top

This pub is over 200 years old and was licensed in the 1800s to sell beer, cider and paraffin. There has been a variety of paranormal occurrences over the years, from ghostly footsteps, glasses thrown across the bar, the moving of tables, fleeting shadowy figures and, on one occasion, a bizarre report of peculiar spears of white light.

The Tickled Trout

This quirkily named pub on the Lower Road probably gets its name from the fact that it sits on the river at West Farleigh, where trout are in abundance. It dates back to 1421 and has experienced several bouts of paranormal activity, to the extent that the team behind the ghost hunting series *Most Haunted* showed an interest in investigating the pub. Several staff have sensed a presence in the cellar and been touched by something unseen. A spiritualist said they were pushed by some unknown presence and others have reported having their ankles grabbed by the spectre. The ghost could be of a coachman, but little else is known.

YALDING

This quaint village boasts the longest medieval bridge in Kent; said to measure 150 yards, it spans two rivers. The Saxon village was called Twyford, but the Domesday records it as the Saxon 'manor of Hallinges owned by Aldret'.

It was also recorded as 'Ge-aeldinge' (the old village) and by 1642 became 'Yaldinge'. The village has been prone to flooding in the past and during the sixteenth century was ravaged by the plague.

Plague Ghosts

Sadly, the village seems reticent to give up its ghostly secrets, and those it does offer are extremely vague. Shadowy forms, infrequently reported, are said to be the ghosts of those who suffered the epidemic. Maybe they still loiter in some kind of limbo, unable to escape the tragedy that befell them and their village centuries ago.

During the 1920s, Edith Nesbit, author of *The Railway Children*, wrote of her fondness of the village, stating, 'The Medway just above the Anchor (at Yalding, Kent) is a river of dreams … If you go to Yalding you may stay at The George and be comfortable in a little village that owns a haunted churchyard…'

The Tickled Trout, West Farleigh.

The author, dressed for the occasion!

…I think the next best step for you all will be home and bed.
'The Haunted Jarvee' by William Hope Hodgson (*Carnacki the Ghost Finder*)

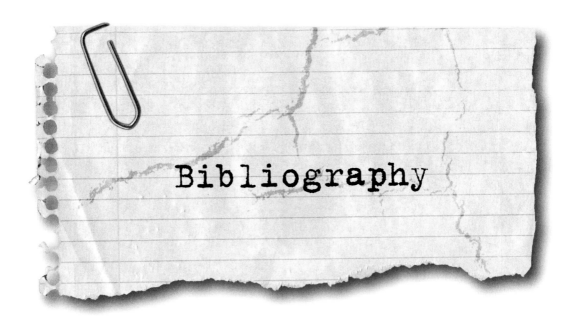

Bibliography

BOOKS

Alexander, M., *Haunted Houses You May Visit* (Sphere, 1982)

Alexander, M., *Haunted Pubs in Britain and Ireland* (Sphere, 1984)

Arnold, N., *Mystery Animals Of The British Isles: Kent* (CFZ Press, 2009)

Bignell, A., *Kent Lore* (Hale, 1983)

Cameron, J., *Haunted Kent* (Tempus, 2005)

Crowe, C., *Night Side of Nature or Ghosts and Ghost Seers* (1848)

Green, A., *Ghosts of the South East* (David & Charles, 1976)

Green, A., *Haunted Kent Today* (S.B. Publications, 1999)

Hewett, R., *Maidstone Official Charter 1549-1949* (1949)

Igglesden, C., *A Saunter Through Kent With Pen and Pencil* (Kentish Express, Various dates)

John, M., *Around Historic Kent* (Midas, 1978)

Kissick, E., *A Steep High Hill* (1996)

Lyon-Playfair, G., *The Haunted Pub Guide,* (Stein & Day, 1985)

Matthews, R., *Ghost Hunter Walks in Kent* (SB Publications, 2005)

O'Donnell, E., *Confessions of a Ghost Hunter* (Butterworth, 1928)

Osborne-Thomason, N., *The Ghost Hunting Casebook* (Blandford, 1999)

Paine, B. & Sturgess, T., *Unexplained Kent* (Breedon Books, 1997)

Prescott-Row, B. & Stanley, M., *Kent's Capital* (Homeland Ass Handbook, 1899)

Sanders, F., *Psychical Research in Haunted Kent: Specially Written For the Society For Psychical Research – Investigations Carried Out Between February 1939 to December 1940* (Privately Published)

Sissons, R., *Single Track Obsession: A Book of Extraordinary Railway Journeys* (Trafford Publishing, 2008)

Spencer, J. & A., *The Encyclopaedia of Ghosts & Spirits* (Headline, 1992)

Thornborough, R., *Exploring Loose Village* (Loose Amenities Association, 1978)

Underwood, P., *Ghosts of Kent* (Meresborough, 1985)

Unknown Author, *Crimes That Shook The Medway Towns* (Parrett & Neves, 1973)

Weaver, G., *Kent Ghosts* (James Pike Ltd, 1977)

WEBSITES

www.burhamvillage.com

www.ghostconnections.co.uk

www.ghostsearch.co.uk

www.historickent.com

www.kentmonsters.blogspot.com

www.leedskent.org.uk

www.oakonthegreen.com

www.paranormaldatabase.com

www.roadghosts.com

www.southernpiteam.co.uk

www.strangetalesfromthedollshouse.blogspot.com

www.thefriars.org.uk

www.villagenet.co.uk

www.wateringburypc.co.uk

www.westfarleigh.org.uk

www.wikipedia.org

Other titles published by The History Press

Haunted Rochester
NEIL ARNOLD & KEVIN PAYNE

The antiquated town of Rochester is riddled with tales of phantom monks, eerie tunnel, romantic spirits, dark apparitions, and eerie history. Now, however, comes a unique volume which proves that Rochester is in fact one of the most haunted places in Britain its High Street alone harbours over forty ghost stories. The atmosphere described by Charles Dickens many years ago can now be seen in a more chilling light, so read on to discover the ghosts of Rochester's past.

978 0 7524 5779 6

Paranormal Kent
NEIL ARNOLD

Kent has long been known as the 'Garden of England', however this idyllic corner of Britain also has its darker side and has a long history of paranormal occurrences. This richly illustrated book covers a fascinating range of strange events. From sightings of Big Cats, UFOs, monsters and fairies, to terrifying tales of dragon encounters and phantom hitchhikers, this incredible volume will invite the reader to view the area in a whole new light. Paranormal Kent will delight all those interested in the mysteries of the paranormal.

978 0 7524 5590 7

Kent Folk Tales
TONY COOPER

These traditional stories and local legends have been handed down by storytellers for centuries. As folk tales reveal a lot about the people who created them, this book provides a link to the ethics and way of life of Kentish people. Here you will find the intriguing tales of King Herla, the Wantsum Wyrm and the Battle of Sandwich, to name but a few. These captivating stories, brought to life with a collection of unique illustrations, will be enjoyed by readers time and again.

978 0 7524 5933 2

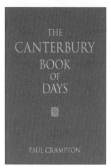

The Canterbury Book of Days
PAUL CRAMPTON

Taking you through the year, day by day, *The Canterbury Book of Days* contains a quirky, eccentric, amusing or important event or fact from different periods of history, many of which had a major impact on the religious and political history of England as a whole. Ideal for dipping into, this addictive little book will keep you entertained and informed. Featuring hundreds of snippets of information gleaned from the vaults of Canterbury's archives, it will delight residents and visitors alike.

978 0 7524 5685 0

Visit our website and discover thousands of other History Press books.

www.thehistorypress.co.uk